Seven Steps to Elevating Effective Prayer

Miracles in the Rockies

By Rex Tonkins

xulon
PRESS

PASTOR REX TONKINS

Rex Tonkins is an ordained minister, but is better known as Coach Rex. He has spent over twenty-eight years helping young people and leaders discover their purpose and destiny in Christ Jesus. Rex is the co-founder and Executive Director of *The Destiny Project,* headquartered in Colorado Springs, Colorado. Rex has traveled extensively around the USA for fifteen years helping young people discover their purpose and destiny, using the platforms of sports camps, sports tournaments and leadership camps.

Rex attended Lenoir Rhyne University on a football scholarship and earned a degree in Sports Management with a minor in Business Management. He also earned a Master's degree in Curriculum and Instruction from the University of Phoenix in 2008.

Rex's leadership background starts with serving as captain of the track team in high school, in college as co-captain of the football team and president of FCA. Rex served as a distribution supervisor for JP Stevens Textile Company after he graduated from Lenoir Rhyne University. He served as youth pastor and auxiliary leader with the late Pastor Otis Lockett, Sr. and he served as a prayer coordinator in the distribution department while employed at Focus on the Family.

Rex coached basketball for over fifteen years on the high school level as well as taught in two school systems for eight years as athletic director and track coach. Rex was the first director of The Malachi House in Greensboro, NC, a home for men with life controlling issues. He also served with Pastor Al Pittman as an associate pastor at Calvary Worship Center in Colorado Springs, CO for over three years. For two consecutive years, he served as prayer leader for National Day of Prayer in Colorado Springs. Rex has assisted with strategic planning to reach young people in multiple cities: Colorado Springs, CO; Denver, CO; Oklahoma City, OK; Clearwater, FL; Lakeland, FL; Atlanta, GA; Hickory, NC; Greensboro, NC; Burlington, NC; Gastonia, NC; Virginia Beach, VA; and Staten Island, NY.

Rex, along with his wife Vickie, has written and published curriculum for young people. He has been married to Vickie for twenty-eight years and they have two beautiful children, Christian, who attended Montreat College in NC on a basketball and academic scholarship, and their daughter, Victoria attended Texas Bible Institute in Columbus, TX.

Email: rex@youhaveadestiny.org

Elevating to Your Destiny

Seven Ways to Elevate Communication with Jesus

By Rex Tonkins

Table of Contents

Introduction

Super Bowl 37

On one hot summer day in August, I met Tony at Western Carolina University. We were both freshman; he played offensive line and I was a running back. Tony made a lasting impression on me because he constantly laughed while I read my Bible. He tried to convince me that I did not need to read the Word and instead invited me to parties with him. I attended Western Carolina for only one semester and would not see Tony again until we talked after a Denver Bronco game almost two decades later.

Tony made his way into the National Football League in an unusual way. He ran stadium steps at Western and a scout from the Cleveland Browns took notice and one opportunity led to another and Tony soon played for the Cleveland Browns. He played for the Browns for eleven seasons and then gained another opportunity to play for the Denver Broncos. When I discovered Tony was the same teammate at Western who played for the Broncos, I made it my goal to get in touch with him at one of the preseason games where Denver played the San Francisco 49ers.

I walked behind the Bronco bench with my two kids, my son Christian and my daughter Victoria and called Tony's name. He turned around with a look like, "Who in the world is calling me?" I said, "This is Rex." He looked at me in amazement and said he needed to speak to me after the game. He said to tell the gatekeeper to allow me in after the game.

When we came into the gate, Tony said, "I have to tell you something. In the Denver Bronco stadium, on the million dollar turf field, I gave my life to Jesus."

I was more excited about this news than attending a football game. This was the beginning of a new adventure with the Bronco organization and our ministry. The Destiny Project gained favor with the Denver Broncos organization. Visiting training camp in Greely and sitting at the training table with the Bronco team, I was impressed Coach Shanahan served members of The Destiny Project ice cream after we ate lunch.

Tony Jones was the door of opportunity that afforded us to bring young people to Bronco games. Tony was number seventy-seven and was the starting offensive left tackle for what is called the blind side. Tony was the main person to cover quarterback blind side. We later connected with the Contemporary Services Corporation (C.S.C.), a security group, to work with organizations to raise funds for The Destiny Project. They were so impressed with our Destiny coaches and work of excellence that they invited our entire team to work a security detail at the Super Bowl in San Diego, California. Super Bowl 37 was the Tampa Bay Buccaneers versus the Oakland Raiders.

We were delighted to be a part of this occasion in February 2003. We joined a group of about seventy security officers who traveled by tour buses to California.

Work began the moment we stepped off the bus; we were assigned roles and quickly mobilized to work the pre-game event. The following day, during the Super Bowl, I had the unique opportunity of meeting many professional athletes as well as movie stars. I was positioned in a place where both teams went on and came off the field. After the game was over and Tampa Bay was declared the Super Bowl Champion, I said, "Be sure to give God the glory."

Some said, "That's right," and others looked at me strangely. One professional who looked at me strangely was a defensive lineman for Tampa Bay. Once I spoke this message to the players, I felt as though my assignment was complete. Immediately afterward, we all loaded the bus to return to Colorado. We left that evening, traveling through the state of Utah to pick up a relief driver to take the second leg into Colorado. We then began our second leg of the journey home.

It was a February morning with snow-capped mountains, between five and six a.m. All passengers were asleep and I heard the Holy Spirit say, "Wake up Rex." I recognized my Father's voice and woke up. I looked out of the window at the snowy Colorado Rockies and noticed the bus was headed toward the edge of the road. In this particular section of the interstate, there were no guardrails, only a steep drop from the road. I looked to my left to see what was going on with the driver. His head lay over to his side; he had fallen asleep at the wheel! I jumped out of my seat from the third row and grabbed the steering wheel to keep the bus on I-70, instead of several hundred feet below. I woke up the driver and told him to pull over at the next exit. I said I wanted the other driver to drive, with whom I felt safer. The sleepy driver listened to me and switched. Whispers could be heard all the way to the back of the bus saying, "He saved our lives by waking up the bus driver." Vickie and I noticed every member on the bus had an appreciative attitude toward us, realizing we had been saved from a fatal disaster.

I have been inspired to write this book because of the many miracles God has demonstrated in my life like the one you just read. The goal of this book is to help equip, encourage and empower people how to hear and talk with Jesus daily. The times we are living in require we have a heightened sense of alertness. When you read the pages of this book, you will be encouraged to elevate your communication with God on an entirely new level.

Nehemiah 4:14 says: "And I looked and arose and said to the nobles, to the leaders, and to the rest of the people, 'Do not be afraid of them. Remember the Lord, great and awesome, and fight for your brethren, your sons, your daughters, and your wives, and your homes.'"

Nehemiah answered the call and mandate to do something about the walls of Jerusalem that were in desolation. Through personal repentance, prayer and courage, Nehemiah rallied the people to take a stand and fight for their country. We as believers must follow the example of Nehemiah and avail ourselves to God's wishes. We are in a war in America and we need to pray as never before. When we hear God's marching orders, we must take action aligning with God's agenda and advance with God's orders. Regardless of circumstances, we must obey God's leading, understanding God wants to use you for His purposes. We must awaken from our stupor as Christ followers and remember we are living in war. John Piper stated, "You will not know what prayer is for, until you know that life is war. Prayer is a tool of warfare."

In O.S. Hillman's book, *Change Agent*, he pinpoints our culture today. This is an analogy that best describes the American church today with the following analogy: "A frog jumped into cool water in a kettle, not feeling the heat had been turned on. Gradually the heat became hot, and the frog did not notice the extreme heat until the frog was burned to death in the kettle." America has been sitting in the kettle of cultural slide into liberalism and it is now beginning to alarm Christ followers to the point that they are ready to do something about it. We must hear the voice of the Holy Spirit to avoid Satan's tactics of attempting to destroy us at every turn. It's time for Christ followers to arise from our stupor.

Joel 3:9-11:

Proclaim this among the nations: Prepare for war! Wakeup the mighty men, Let all the men draw near, let them come up. Beat your plowshares into swords and your pruning hooks into spears. Let the weak say, I am strong. Assemble and come, all you nations, and gather together all around. Cause Your mighty ones to go down there, O Lord.

We must be prepared prayerfully for difficult challenges as Christ followers. We will need the power of the Holy Spirit to help us excel in the days ahead. Despite the difficult times, we have a great door of opportunity to advance God's work. **Jesus said, "In the world you will have tribulation. But be of good cheer! I have overcome the world" (John 16:33).**

The model Jesus gave us is in **Matthew 6:9-13:**

> **In this manner therefore pray: Our Father in heaven, hallowed be Your name. Your Kingdom come. Your will be done on earth as it is in heaven. Give us this day our daily bread. And forgive us our debts as we forgive our debtors. And do not lead us into temptation, but deliver us from the evil one. For yours is the kingdom and the power forever, Amen.**

The first verse deals with recognizing God as Father and holy. Secondly, "Give us this day our daily bread," is asking God for specific provision spiritually, emotionally and physically. "Thy Kingdom come," points to God desiring His will manifesting in the earth. "Forgive us as we forgive our debtors," deals with relationships and heart issues. "Lead us not into temptation," is asking God to direct your steps, and "deliver us from evil." "Yours is the kingdom," means all power and authority originates from God. This model is the foundation for prayer and I will take you through elevating prayer points that have been proven over time to get results.

In this book, I breakdown each chapter with the following titles: Private Times of Prayer, God's Remarkable Divine Intervention, The Authority God has Given to the Believer, A Life Yielded Allows us to Cooperate with the Holy Spirit, Time with God Empowers us for Great Exploits, Being Ready Allows Us to be Used in Miracle Moments, and having God's strategy allows us to operate under God's divine timing and strategy to win victories for God's kingdom. "Prayer" is defined as: "a solemn request for help or expression of thanks to God." *Strong's*

Concordance (4336) *proseuchomai* means "I pray, pray for, offer prayer" (pros toward, exchange) (*euxomai* to wish, pray, properly exchange wishes), "to literally interact with the Lord by switching human wishes for His wishes as God imparts faith to us."

Matthew 6:33: "But seek first the kingdom of God and His righteousness, and all these things shall be added unto you."

The day I accepted Jesus as my personal savior, I knew I was involved in something amazing. I experienced a different kind of love. God's love is accepting and affirming. Prior to receiving Jesus, I was on a road of destruction, running the streets late hours of the night and involved in gang activity. Many of my associates went to prison and many peers died around me. I recognized if I did not make a change, I would suffer the same fate. My way out of the gang came on a fall day somewhere around September where the principal at Grimsley High School gave us a mandate that demanded gangs such as ours, called the "Scorpions," could not wear gang clothes to school. During the same time, I had a lot of success with football. Schools like Clemson and East Carolina expressed interest in me.

I went to the gang leader and said, "I will comply with the demand because I have opportunities for my future."

The gang leader said, "You do what you have to do, but no one will tell us what to do."

Looking back, that decision was a day of destiny for me and a day of destruction for the friends with whom I once ran. Being in the gang, I did not know I sought affirmation. The places I searched brought pain, despair and disappointment.

When I asked Jesus into my life, I experienced a love, acceptance and affirmation like I had never known. Knowing Jesus Christ helped me survive and overcome in an inner city environment where crime and violence was a daily occurrence. **Psalm 16:8 (NLT): "I know the Lord is always with me. I will not be shaken, for He is right beside me."**

In this book, I will reveal keys that have empowered my life for leadership, sports, ministry and life. The Holy Spirit guides us through every situation we ask for help; the Holy Spirit is our guide to making a connection with Jesus. I will share God's treasures that pulled me out of darkness and placed me on a road of purpose. The best way to describe prayer, from my vantage point, is to fall in love with Jesus and talk with Him with of all your heart. Reveal intimate secrets of your heart. Share fears, frustrations and dreams with Him.

Prior to receiving Christ, many of my decisions led me in the direction of destruction. My reality is I could have died without knowing Jesus as my savior and spent eternity in hell. Thanks be to God for His marvelous grace. At the age of twelve, I came to understand I needed God to help me change direction, from destruction to destiny and purpose in Christ.

John 15:5 states, "I am the vine, you are the branches. He who abides in Me, and I in him, bears much fruit. For without me you can do nothing."

The keyword here is "nothing." Nothing means "Something that has no quantitative value; zero, something that has no substance." When we are living for Jesus, and aligned with God's agenda, we advance God's kingdom. We involve ourselves in a redemptive purpose to help people have life and life more fulfilling.

When we are living our life for Jesus, we gain insight to advance the kingdom of God, and help people understand how to live victoriously in Christ Jesus. People are oppressed by Satan, which causes them to lose hope, destroying their lives and the lives of others. Jesus came to set captives free and we are God's vessels to help free people from the deception of our enemy. It is imperative that we seek God so we can help bring hope and healing to our communities.

Dr. Luke stated in **Luke 18:1, "Then He spoke a parable to them, that men always ought to pray and not lose heart**." When we make prayer a lifestyle, we will have power and courage to push forward in difficult times. Prayer infuses us with fortitude to fight until we obtain victory.

God created us to love Him with all of our heart, mind, soul and strength. When we love God, we come to learn how much God loves us and how He loves all souls. God places great value in people, truth and righteousness. He does not want His people to suffer for unjust causes, being deceived by Satan's lies and wickedness ruling our nation and world. It is imperative that we increase our prayer life to be equipped with power and discernment to overcome difficult days.

1 Timothy 4:1: "Now the Spirit expressly says that in latter times some will depart from the faith, giving heed to deceiving spirits and doctrines of demons."

Matthew 24:24: "For false christs, and false prophets will rise and show great signs and wonders to deceive, if possible, even the elect."

I am emphasizing that Christ followers develop a consistent prayer and devotional life. We must learn to be sensitive to the leading of the Holy Spirit so as to avoid being deceived. **The Bible clearly gives a description of the times ahead in 2 Timothy 3:1-6:**

> **But know this that in the last days perilous times will come: For men will be lovers of themselves, lovers of money, boasters, proud, blasphemers, disobedient to parents, unthankful, unholy, unloving, unforgiving, slanderers, without self-control, brutal, despisers of good, traitors, headstrong, haughty, lovers of pleasure rather than lovers of God, Having a form of godliness but denying its power.**

How can we avoid such volatile times? First, through humbling ourselves in prayer, turning from our wicked ways and seeking God's face. The power of prayer aligns our heart, mind and spirit with God's heart and mind. Let's take a look at each category and compare if we see these characteristics today.

* Love themselves Y/N (Selfish in nature)

* Boasters Y/N (Means an empty pretender; Greek *alazon*)

* Blasphemers Y/N (Speaking evil, slanderous and abusive)

* Proud Y/N (High opinion of themselves)

* Disobedient to parents Y/N (Not compliant)

* Unthankful Y/N

* Unholy Y/N (wicked)

* Without natural affection Y/N (Unsociable)

* False accusers Y/N (prone to slander)

*   Without self-control Y/N

*   Traitors Y/N (Betrayer)

*   High-minded Y/N (reckless)

*   Lovers of pleasure more than lovers of God Y/N (loving pleasure will be distinctly greater)

I am amazed that people's love for pleasure will not compare, by far. Pleasure will take a front seat more than loving Jesus in times ahead.

Now take a journey with me through *Elevating to Your Destiny through Prayer* and allow the Holy Spirit to speak to you as you read these valuable biblical truths. Christ followers, don't give world news your best part of waking, but give God your first and best to get His perspective of the world today. We have a rendezvous with the Father every morning to receive divine communication from the throne as how to advance His work. I like what the late Ronald Reagan stated once in a speech:

> You and I have a rendezvous with destiny. We will preserve for our children this, the last best hope of man on earth, or we sentence them to take the first step into a thousand years of darkness. If we fail, at least let our children and their children say of us, we justified a brief moment here. We did all that could be done.

We have a responsibility to fight for righteousness in the culture, so that generations to come can enjoy the freedom to live for Jesus. Ronald Reagan also stated:

Freedom is never more than one generation away from extinction. We didn't pass it to our children in the blood stream. It must be fought for protected and handed on for them to do the same, or one day we will spend our sunset years telling our children and our children's children what it was like in the United States where men were free and revered God.

Matthew 6:33: "Seek first the kingdom of God and His righteousness and all these things will be added unto you." As we seek God, He will show us ways to elevate above these cultural mindsets that are prevalent today. Seeking God will empower us to do righteous acts of love and kindness in our world. Many individuals in our world have been deprived of love and discipline. First, the Greek word *proton*, meaning "firstly in time, place, in order of importance." It also means "before, at the beginning, order of importance." John Eckhardt, in his book *50 Truths*, points out when an individual first wakes in the morning, his or her mind is the sharpest. I believe we should give God the best part of waking on a daily basis by praising Him and through study and meditation of the scriptures. In addition, before we get going with our busy lives, we should seek God regarding His agenda for that day, so we can be prepared with fresh insight.

Experiencing Keys of Effective Prayer

Review

1. What was the key in the people surviving a potentially fatal accident?
2. Why should we seek first the kingdom of God?

3. How can we be effective in producing fruit according to John 15:5?

4. What will happen in the last times according 1 Timothy 4:1?

5. How will people behave in the culture according to 2 Timothy 3:1-6?

6. Will you make a commitment to pray more than you ever have?

7. Why did I write this book?

Look at what you are facing in your own life.

_____

_____

_____

_____

Make a small commitment and build your prayer and devotional life. Example: commit to pray first thing in the morning for seven minutes. Ask God to help you develop the discipline to pray consistently. Identify what hinders you from seeking God. Ask God for guidance in overcoming obstacles to praying daily.

Suggested Reading:

Nehemiah 1

Matthew 6

Proverbs 3

Step One: Private

Matthew 6:6:

"But when you pray, go into your room, and when you have shut your door, pray to your Father who is in secret place; and your Father who sees in secret will reward you openly."

In step one, a private place is important, especially to giving God your undivided attention. Be aware there are many forces that attempt to pull us away from intimacy with God. Intimacy with God is sharing our inner secrets, dealing with the deepest areas of our soul that often come up when we face a crisis. In these private moments is when these issues should be dealt with; God already knows the secrets of our heart. Confessing and sharing them will help us grow to maturity.

Oswald Chambers said, "It is impossible to conduct my life as a disciple without definite times of secret prayer." Private prayer produces powerful people to propel God's primary purpose.

Step One: Private means: secluded from sight, presence, or intrusion of others. To develop a private prayer life with the Lord, we must develop the discipline of intentionality. This requires we schedule times with God and have the determination to follow through in order to gain an effective prayer life. When we establish this discipline, we will have a life of communion and fellowship with the Holy Spirit who will empower us to live victoriously. Be mindful that our enemy, Satan, often finds ways to intrude on our time and especially our time with the Lord. It is vital that we prioritize time with the Lord on a daily basis to have communion with God. O.S. Hillman stated: "God must take us into isolation in order to give us the privilege of being used for the kingdom. Isolation changes us and removes things that hinder us. God uses isolation to force us to draw deep upon His grace."

Psalm 91:1: "He that dwells in the secret place of the Most high shall abide under the shadow of the Almighty."

When we find that secret place in God, we develop protection over our lives that give us the power to deal with life's pressures. When we learn to praise God in our private time, we experience intimacy and understanding of God's heart that elevates us to new places in Him. **Ephesians 2:5-6**: "Even when we were dead in trespasses, made us alive together with Christ (by grace you have been saved), and raised us up together, and made us sit together in the heavenly places in Christ Jesus." Prayer and worship gives us the ability to be seated in the heavenly realm with Jesus and gain perspective from God's point of view. **Revelation 4:1-2** (NLT):

Then as I looked, I saw a door standing open in heaven, and the same voice I heard before spoke to me like a trumpet blast. The voice said, "Come up here, and I will show you what must happen after this." And instantly I was in the Spirit and I saw a throne in heaven and someone sitting on it.

In this text, God calls John to come up and reveal many mysteries of the kingdom too incredible for the natural mind to comprehend, but made known through the Holy Spirit.

Consistency is a foundational key to elevating your prayer life.

We may not always experience the things we want and desire in prayer immediately, but faithfulness is what brings the breakthrough we need. A persistent obedience is required and necessary to experience satisfaction in your prayer life. **Luke 18:1: "Then He spoke a parable to them, that men ought always pray and not lose heart."** When we look at life and the circumstances that surround us, we can easily become discouraged or lose heart. However, in the midst of life's problems, we must pray God's Word into the circumstances and stay consistent in meditating on the fresh bread we receive from the throne room of heaven. For example, when cutting down a large tree, it requires many attempts before the tree comes down. When we keep on chopping the tree, it will eventually come down. It works the same way in prayer. We must keep praying or chopping until the answer comes. **Matthew 7:7-8: "Ask, and it will be given to you; seek, and you will find; knock, and it will be opened to you. For everyone who asks receives, and**

he who seeks finds, and to him who knocks it will be opened." An important key to prayer is abiding in the word of God and praying in accordance to His will.

My wife, Vickie, came to Jesus as the age of fifteen. She endured much persecution from her family because of her faith. She remained steadfast to see each of her six brothers, parents, aunts and uncles come to Jesus. She prayed for fourteen years for their salvation before the first member of her family came to Christ. This is another example of why consistent prayer is vital! In hearing this testimony, I want to encourage you to commit to pray more consistently and fervently. Watch and wait on God to move on your behalf. Vickie has been a faithful prayer warrior since I have known her.

I recall in 1992 when she witnessed a dramatic and victorious answer to prayer. Vickie's brother Phillip served in the Persian Gulf War in the 90's. He was the chief aboard the U.S.S. Tarwa. It's the navy's amphibious assault ship. Its called, "the eagle of the sea." This battleship was heavily involved in action during the Persian Gulf War and returned to port in 1992. Vickie often wrote letters to her oldest brother explaining how one can become a Christian. We discovered her brother would return from war and Vickie felt strongly that we should go to San Diego. Vickie started praying for provision to be there for the return of the troops. Travel for three people was quite expensive.

A friend told Vickie to speak to an airline attendant, who attended our church. The friend said this attendant may be able to help us. Vickie spoke to the flight attendant and she was able to get us three round-trip tickets for eighty-eight dollars. Her only request was that we not share with anyone how we received the tickets.

Off we went to San Diego to be a part of welcoming our troops home. Vickie's brother had no idea we would be there. When we finally united with Phillip, along with his wife, son, daughter and our son, Phillip, they were greatly surprised to see us. If I remember correctly, this was on a Thursday that he arrived into the port in San Diego. When we arrived back at their home in San Diego, Phillip began to cry uncontrollably because of all he saw in war. He knew God's hand had protected their ship!

Phillip went to church with us on the following Sunday and we all hoped he would answer the call to come to Christ at the end of the service. However, disappointedly, he did not. My wife was heartbroken, but continued to believe God. He told us of a situation that he knew the hand of God protected their ship. He explained the ship was docked next to an area that was loaded with explosives and a scud missile almost hit their ship. It landed between the dock and the ship. As a result Phillip was ready to receive Jesus Christ as his Lord and Savior. Vickie had the awesome honor of leading her brother to Christ in 1992. We then led him to receive the baptism in the Holy Spirit, which empowered him to overcome many obstacles in his life. Phillip has also answered the call to preach and is an ordained minister today. The price of private prayer prepares you for moments like Vickie experienced back in 1992.

Elevating Moment

I have encouraged my family and friends to commit to pray at a designated time daily at the beginning of each morning. Since I have encouraged my family and friends to pray more, I have noticed how this basic discipline has helped many develop a consistent life of prayer.

"As you become increasingly aware of His presence, you will find it easier to discern the way you should go," Sarah Young states in her book *Jesus Calling*.

Beginning your day alone with Me (being Jesus) is essential preparation for success. Relax with Me (being Jesus) while I ready you for action. Quietness is the classroom where you learn to hear my voice. When you realize that your mind has wandered away from me, don't be alarmed or surprised. You live in a world that has been rigged to distract you. Each time you plow your way through the massive distractions to communicate with me, you achieve victory.

Well put by Sarah. I highly recommend this book for everyone, whether a couple or single. What an amazing truth revealed to Sarah because of a life of honesty and transparency with the one who knows everything about us.

1 Thessalonians 5:17 says, "Pray without ceasing." Prayer must be an ongoing lifestyle, not a once in a while activity. **Proverbs 23:26: "My son, give me your heart and let your eyes observe my ways."** Giving your heart means sharing your secret intimate thoughts with God. In my journey of faith, I have vented my fears, frustrations and concerns for the future to God. An important key is God wants us to be honest and transparent with Him. He already knows our heart and thoughts. This honesty helps us become intimate with the Lord by telling Him what is going on inside your heart.

1 Chronicles 28:9:

As for you, my son Solomon, know the God of your father, and serve Him with a loyal heart and with a willing mind; for the Lord searches all hearts and understands all the intent of the thoughts. If you seek Him, He will be found by you; but if you forsake Him, He will cast you off forever.

God knows our motives and why we do the things we do. God understands the decisions whether the decisions and choices are good or bad. When we are still and quiet enough to allow God to reveal our motives, we can address the issues with Him and receive the strength and grace to change our mind about our actions as well as mindsets that are contrary to God's Word. These moments are pivotal in helping us work out our salvation with fear and trembling.

In the book, *For God Sake Rest,* by James Anderson, he states: **"Inability to be still and quiet on the outside may indicate a disturbance on the inside."** Busyness helps one avoid problems and issues in one's life and family. Amazingly enough, we deceive ourselves into thinking problems will go way with much production. The acronym for busy is **B**eing **U**nder **S**atan's **Y**oke (Author unknown). If we are too busy to spend quality time with the one who knows all things, we will find ourselves in the yoke of sin. The Bible says in **Psalm 46:10, "Be still and know that I am God; I will be exalted among the nation, I will be exalted in the earth."**

Elevating Moment:

Stop a moment to calm your mind and emotions, find a solitary place, like Jesus did, so you can hear God's voice. God will give you understanding in how you should deal with issues in your heart and the difficult challenges you are facing in this season of your journey. Many mistakes happen when we are rushed and do not take time to wait for instructions and directions from the Lord. If we don't stop, God has a way of stopping us, so all we can do is look up to Him.

I had orthoscopic knee surgery in January 2014. With these types of surgeries I have seen individuals up and going within days. To my surprise, I had unusual swelling. The doctor's orders were to stay off my feet and elevate my leg for two weeks. I must honestly confess I had a problem with this order because I like to be on the move, being about advancing the kingdom of God. However, this time was a strategic season to receive precise instructions from the Lord.

I recall, in my college days, God allowed circumstances that cause me to be still and alone with Him. A.W. Tozer stated, "It is doubtful whether God can bless a man greatly until He has hurt him deeply." Oftentimes, God is preparing us for change and transition and we don't want to accept what God is showing us. Because He loves us so much, He allows us to go through trials that will draw us toward Him. John Anderson states, "This disturbance may reflect anxiety generated by a lack of trust in objects or person's worthy of trust."

While away on a prayer journey to Florissant, CO in the fall of 2013, I anticipated an awesome time of direction and instruction with and from the Lord. The Lord had a different agenda that day, which totally shocked me and shook my faith to the core. God's agenda was to deal with the issue of unhealthy trust in man and ministry that was deeply embedded in my heart. God revealed that I often over-worked out of fear of not having enough. I humbled myself and sat on the ground. The Lord did laser surgery on my heart. Sad, but true, I lacked trust and faith in God to fully take care of me. I cried for hours, totally broken, and allowed God into areas of brokenness that stemmed all the way back to the age of seven.

The way to elevate to your destiny is to allow God to take you into the oper-ation room of isolation. After having this scheduled time away, I understood why I was so driven toward doing ministry and not driven to seek God fully. I tried to control every aspect of life and ministry and had allowed pride and fear to blind me from putting complete trust in God. This kind of mindset was rooted from my childhood of experiencing rejection and abandonment. I made a vow at age seven that I would take care of myself, since I could not depend on my loved ones to help me and protect me. I obviously did not get the necessary discipline and nur-turing that is vital in training young men to be productive citizens. I have made a choice to release and forgive those in my family who seemed not to be there when I needed them as a child. Despite it all, God's grace was and is sufficient to help me be an overcomer, not a victim of my circumstances.

In the Lord's Prayer, Jesus said, "forgive us of our debts as we forgive our debtors." In private prayer times with God, we learn how to release those who hurt us and those we have hurt. Forgiveness means, "I am willing to accept the consequences of someone else's sin or bad decisions." There are too many people walking around who are not in touch with their pain and past. Forgiveness does not automatically remove or reverse the consequences imposed by a careless or evil act. In life, having a heart of forgiveness is essential for fostering a tender heart of love. **Ephesians 4:32: "And be kind to one another, tenderhearted, forgiving one another, even as God in Christ also forgave you,"** is vital to having a forgiving heart. In private prayer, God gives us the ability to release the pain and helps us be still enough to face and deal with the issues.

In John Anderson's book, *For God's Sake Rest,* he states "**Perhaps the greatest temptation we face is the temptation to ignore private moments which prepare us for making right decisions in public**. During private prayer time, we can ask a series of questions such as from where this thought originated" (Anderson, 213). Is the thought from the Holy Spirit signaling us to deal with a specific area in our life and past or is the thought coming from Satan who often tries to defeat us in our thought life? We need to be in touch with God so that we can know what God wants to reveal to us. When we develop consistent fellowship with Jesus, we will live a victorious spirit filled life. "Power comes out of stillness; strength comes out of solitude. Decisions that change the entire course of your life come out of the Holy of Holies, your stillness before God" (Anderson, 181). "Look around and be distressed, look inside and be depressed, look at Jesus and be at rest."

Psalm 37:4 (The Message): "Get away with me and you'll recover your life."

Private moments with God give us a glimpse of how good God truly is and when we receive the urgency of life with Him, we can be positioned to gain revelation of His glory and kingdom plan. As I close this chapter, I want to share with you why private prayer is vital. Having a set and consistent time with God gives you a fresh perspective each day. You learn to see life from God's point of view, which is the correct vantage point.

I recall during my college days, my special times of prayer and praise with the Lord on Friday afternoons. I went to the chapel and shared my heart with the Lord and He shared His wonderful and glorious heart with me concerning my future and destiny. Let me tell you, God is holy and awesome. Don't miss out on how awesome He is. During my college years, I learned to build a close friendship with the King of kings and Lord of lords.

I also recall my season of brokenness when I tore my Anterior Cruciate Ligament (referred often as ACL) and Medial Collateral Ligament (MCL) with playing college football at Lenoir Rhyne University in my senior season with two games remaining in my college career. I was angry with God and did not understand why He allowed this to happen to me.

O.S. Hillman speaks of the valley of *baca* in Hebrew, meaning "to weep; to bemoan." He says every great leader will pass through the valley of *baca*. God ministered to me and poured His precious anointing oil into to my pain and grief. I could feel God's loving presence and affirmation during that time in my life. My plan was to play in the World Football League, which was called NFL Europe in the late 80's and 90's. After months of rehab on my knee, I attended a scout camp in Atlanta on the campus of Georgia Tech University. I pulled a hamstring and was bothered with another setback. I was still offered an opportunity to join a team. I chose not to further my football career because of this rough time of injuries as a running back.

My wife felt I should have played. I probably should have, but I was the one who had endured the pain and suffering during and after games. After some games, my head and entire body were sore. I probably had concussions, but was not aware of concussion like symptoms in the 80's, how ironic. I thought about my future health and wanted to be healthy enough to be involved with my children when they play sports. I had teammates who now have many issues with their health due to playing football. I remember one former teammate who suffered multiple knee injuries and surgeries and could barely walk. He did his college report on knee injuries. He wore shorts to class that day and explained each surgery and how it was performed. This definitely made a lasting impression on me. In modern-day medicine, the procedure for knee surgeries is much better than in the mid-80's and 90's. My point here is life is hard sometimes, but when we turn to God for help, we express our real heart and thoughts with a holy God. He will help us through difficult seasons of our life especially when we feel like giving up.

Learning private prayer, I want to turn my attention to leaders, Pastor Steve and Balinda. This couple demonstrated the love of Christ to me while in college and they modeled Christ's love in a way I have rarely seen demonstrated by someone who was not a part of my immediate family. Through the love of Christ, they cared for me in a way that added value and affirmation to me as a young naïve college student. This family modeled what private prayer is supposed to look like.

In my home, as a young child, I did not see prayer as a priority. The pastors opened their heart and home to this young college student, which helped me see the importance of prayer. I was like little Samuel, learning to discern and respond to the voice of God. Their relationship with Christ helped me understand when we seek God and wait on God to speak to us we gain insight into what God is leading us to do. I watched these mentors sit quietly, read scriptures, sing praises, take authority over the enemy with the sword of the word of God and make declarations that empowered them for service unto the Lord. After seeing the effectiveness of private prayer, I put prayer to practice when we moved to my hometown, Greensboro, NC in October 1989 to serve as youth pastor for the late Bishop Otis Lockett, Sr.

I remember the time vividly because North Carolina experienced one of the worst hurricanes since I was born, Hurricane Hugo. Because of the leadership responsibilities appointed to me, I knew I needed to connect in prayer to be an effective husband, father and leader.

I worked as a supervisor at a textile company in the shipping and receiving department overseeing twenty employees. This assignment was one of the toughest assignments of my young career. I knew I had to make a commitment to be involved in early morning prayer at the church and sometimes noonday prayer. I needed help dealing with difficult people and confidence in my ability to handle responsibly for millions of manufacturing goods coming in and out of the distribution center. This time and season of prayer was foundational to experiencing success in my job as supervisor and a youth pastor of a fast-growing church.

During my private prayer times with the Lord, He gave me so many creative ideas to encourage young people and parents during the early 90's. I give God praise for the young people who are now adults, who to this day talk about how glorious those days were for their development and knowledge of Christ. I am honored and blessed to see those who were a part of the "unshakable" youth group and are now serving God in ministry and in their workplace.

Private prayer produces powerful people. **Luke 5:15-17:**

> **However, the report went around concerning Him all the more; and great multitudes came together to hear, and to be healed by Him of their infirmities. So He Himself often withdrew into the wilderness and prayed. Now it happened on a certain day, as He was teaching that there were Pharisees and teachers of the law sitting by, who had come out of every town of Galilee, Judea, and Jerusalem. And the power of the Lord was present to heal them.**

If you notice, Jesus withdrew often to be alone with God and when He returned, the scripture says there was the power of the Lord to heal them. Jesus did many power moves coming out of prayer.

In **Mark 6:45-51**, after Jesus fed the five thousand:

> **Immediately after this, Jesus insisted that his disciples get back into the boat and head across the lake to Bethsaida, while he sent people home. After telling everyone good-bye, he went up into the hills by himself to pray. Late that night, the disciples were in their boat in the middle of the lake, and Jesus was alone on land. He saw that they were in serious trouble, rowing hard and struggling against the wind and waves. About three o'clock in the morning Jesus came toward them, walking on the water.**

He intended to go past them, but when they saw him walking on the water, they cried out in terror, thinking he was a ghost. They were all terrified when they saw him. But Jesus spoke to them don't be afraid, He said, "Take courage! I am here!" Then he climbed into the boat and the wind stopped. They were totally amazed.

When we ask Jesus into our situation, He can calm things down and leaves us with peace.

Elevating Moment:

I recall an incident on my college campus. An athletic trainer nicknamed "Big E" was about six feet four inches. Big E had a problem with hiccups that lasted for days. I had to visit his office that particular day and he began to share how uncomfortable he had been. I asked if I could pray for him. He said yes. I took my right hand, put it on his chest and prayed, "In the name of Jesus, hiccups be gone." Instantly, the hiccups went away. He became emotional and amazed by the power of God.

Experiencing Elevated Private Prayer
Review

1. Why should you get alone with God to pray?

2. How can you give God your heart?

3. How does God desire you to treat people according to Ephesians 4:32?

4. According Psalm 46:10, why do we need to develop times of stillness?

5. What did you learn from coach Rex's private prayer times?

6. What do you think Jesus talked to God about in their private times?

7. How can we experience more power as a Christ follower?

What keeps you busy?

_____

_____

_____

_____

Prayers to Pray:

_____

_____

_____

_____

Suggested Reading:

Psalm 46

Matthew 6

Luke 5

The Move to Colorado

The inspiration to move to Colorado was conceived in private prayer. In developing a daily prayer life, I could recognize more clearly the voice of God and impressions from reading scripture to which the Lord directed me. I also believe it is important to be submitted to spiritual authority and to ask your leaders to pray with you regarding God's holy endeavors for your life. I believe accountability helps one avoid destructibility.

I have come to realize, over the years, when God gives you instruction, it is not always to be done right now. His timing is an important part of the process. Waiting on God is the key for God's timing of when you should transition into the new place where He is calling you.

I remember praying in the sanctuary one Tuesday evening at Evangel Fellowship Church on Balboa Street in Greensboro, NC. I said, "Lord show me what to do so I can do it."

That is when I heard the Lord say into my spirit, "Colorado."

In amazement, I said, "If this is you Lord, please confirm."

The Lord gave so many undeniable confirmations that we knew God had spoken to us. One last and final confirmation came while attending a youth conference in Virginia Beach, VA. The speaker's message came from **Acts 9:6: "So he, trembling and astonished said, 'Lord, what you want me to do?' Then the Lord said to him, 'Arise and go into the city, and you will be told what you must do.'"** God impressed this scripture upon my heart. This was the scripture that I aligned my heart with in prayer.

During this conference I received a word of wisdom, based on 1 Corinthians 12, through one of the speakers. He could have only known about this by the Spirit of God. What God spoke to me in private was confirmed publicly. I believe, when we are hungry for God and pursue Him, He is faithful to reveal His will to us.

Elevating Moment:

Another private prayer moment came in the way I became employed at Focus on the Family, who at the time employed 1,500 people. I put my application in for employment and the HR department told me the process would take three weeks for an interview. I said okay and began to further my search for work the following day in a city called Castle Rock, CO, located about thirty minutes from Colorado Springs. When I arrived at the location, to my disappointment, I had arrived the wrong day to test for the job for the State. I was bothered because of the waste of time and fuel.

While making the drive back to Colorado Springs, I sensed the Lord telling me to go back to Focus on the Family. I in turn told the Lord, "They said three weeks." I had this argument with Lord, and I yielded to the Lord and went back to Focus on the Family.

When I arrived, the H.R. director entered at the same time and I asked about my application. She asked about when I had filled out the application.

I said, "Yesterday."

Lisa Crump reiterated that the process takes three weeks. I said to her, "I need the favor of God."

To my surprise, by the time I arrived home, I received a call for an interview and was hired immediately. Case in point, when we yield to God's voice, we will see power move. He will open doors and elevate us to places in Him. Knowing and hearing the voice of God is the most important asset you can have. It is more important than any career, success or fame.

While working at Focus on the Family I had to arrive early with only one family car. I car-pooled with a neighbor, who had to be at work two hours earlier. I decided to use this time in the Focus on the Family prayer chapel. During this private prayer time, the Lord spoke to me about launching the ministry of The Destiny Project at a Doherty high school. The key again to hearing God's voice is the consistency of private prayer time. I am to this day thankful to Lisa Crump, the H.R. representative, for allowing the Lord to use her as a vessel to propel me into my destiny. She has served as the mobilization leader for prayer with the National Day of Prayer task force.

Elevating Moment:

During the time I worked for Focus on the Family, I received an invitation from a leader to speak to a group of men and youth at Praise Mountain positioning me to experience a higher level of prayer and solitude geographically and spiritually. I thought the mountains of North Carolina had great views and were high in elevation. However, going to Praise Mountain located in Colorado was not only higher in elevation, but magnificently beautiful. The quiet made my ears ring. I had never experienced that level of stillness and quiet. This was the start of a new level of private prayer. I learned quickly that there were guidelines for attending this retreat—one was that we had to fast. I was fascinated by the solitude and beauty of this place and how I could give the Lord my undivided attention. I was so fascinated with the quietness of this place that I began to schedule more times throughout the year to pray at Praise Mountain. The Lord imparted many impressions, revelations and directions concerning my life and family.

I vividly remember the Lord instructing me to launch our ministry into the nations to evangelize young people through sports and drama. I had no idea that this time in private prayer would reveal strategies to birth hundreds of youth and families into the kingdom of God. We have had an incredible move of God since 2001 reaching young people with the Gospel of Jesus Christ. God has used The Destiny Project sports camps and tours to help young people find purpose and direction for their lives. We have reached out to youth through The Destiny Project since 1997. If I had not already understood the importance of private prayer, I would have missed opportunities to discover God's agenda for each season of my life.

A.W. Tozer prayed:

> Lord, teach me to listen. The times are noisy and my ears are weary
> with the thousand raucous sounds which continuously assault them.
> Give me the spirit of the boy Samuel when he said to thee, "Speak,
> for thy servant heareth." Let me hear Thee speaking in my heart.
> Let me get used to the sound of Thy voice, that its tones may be
> familiar. Amen.

Elevating Moment:

The point I want to make here is when you develop a private prayer life and practice a lifestyle of private prayer, you are able to discern God's voice in crucial moments. God saved us on that snowy day in Colorado simply because one person heard the voice of God. If I had not been alert to God's voice, I wouldn't be writing this book to tell the story. I am so thankful God helped me respond in a timely fashion. How often do we miss those moments because we don't listen or respond to God? He is speaking to us, but are we listening and yielding to God? Your prayer life is the most powerful force on earth. Prayer changes outcomes.

Satan has a goal to kill, steal and destroy every person, especially the Christ follower! Jesus came to give us life to live more abundantly. We need the fortitude and discipline of Daniel, especially in the days in which we live. Life in America and around the globe is much more volatile. Daniel experienced divine invasions because he was committed to what I call "triple threat prayer." Daniel prayed three times a day and became a threat to the kingdom of darkness. Daniel did not allow the customs and laws to dictate when, where and whom he should honor. He remained faithful to pray to a living God (Daniel 6:10).

Caleb also experienced strong faith in God because he knew God more intimately. The Bible says Caleb had a different spirit that set him apart from the others (Numbers 14:24). I have witnessed private prayer sets us apart for higher purposes. If you desire satisfaction in your walk with God, then you must put some effort, energy and action into seeking God. First, develop a regular scheduled time to meet with God. Secondly, select a quiet place free of distractions. Thirdly, read scripture, listening for impressions from God. Fourthly, write down the impressions and ponder the thoughts God has given you. Finally, ask God what His agenda is for the day; listen and wait.

The Latin word *satis*, from the word "satisfaction," means "enough or adequate." If you have enough action toward the things of God, you will experience satisfaction in God. Satisfaction means the fulfillment of one's wishes, expectations or needs. God is the one who meets our deepest needs and when we release our expectations to God, He exceeds them. God wishes above all things that we be in health and prosper even as our soul prospers (3 John 1:2). To prosper in Greek is *euddoo*. To be successful and healthy in Greek is *hygiaino*, free from any mixture of error, to be sound, to be well, and in good health. God wants us to be successful, free from error, and healthy spiritually, emotionally and physically. I believe a life led by the Holy Spirit can help us achieve God's wish.

Experiencing Elevated Private Prayer
Review

1. How does Rex and Vickie's story correlate to Paul's story in Acts 9:6?

2. How does Isaiah 1:19 relate to Coach Rex being hired at Focus on the Family in a short time?

3. How did Coach Rex know they were in danger while riding on the bus returning from the Super Bowl?

4. How did Daniel maintain courage and excellence in a Babylonian society?

5. Where did Caleb and Joshua get confidence to believe to conquer giants?

6. What is God's desire for the Christ follower?

7. What spoke to you in this chapter?

What you are facing in your own life today?

_____

_____

_____

_____

Suggested Reading:

Acts 9

Daniel 6

Numbers 14:24

Step Two: Remarkable

Jeremiah 33:3 (NLT)

"Ask me and I will tell you remarkable secrets

you do not know about things to come."

Remarkable means worthy of notice, unusual and exceptional. The key that helped me find direction was appropriating God's focus. He birthed in me a vision of playing sports and pursuing my education. Proverbs 29:18 states, "Where there is no vision or revelation the people perish or cast off restraint." Vision, in Hebrew, is *chazon*, meaning sight, dream or revelation. Perish means to run wild, unrestrained.

A preacher saw my future by speaking prophetically to me by saying, "You will play football." This prophetic word was the beginning of gaining vision for my future. Before salvation and the impartation of this prophetic word, I was a young adolescent who had no vision and ran unrestrained. When Jesus came into my life, I began to make changes in my attitude and desires. I received from the

Lord unusual motivation and divine insight to do something positive. When I reached high school, the Lord helped me meet academic requirements, enabling me to go to college.

Inspired by a strong desire to train rigorously, I earned a full football scholarship. By the grace of God, I have been able to accomplish these goals. God filled my heart with remarkable insight and revelation of what He wanted to do in this young boy from the inner city. Only God could have given me the vision and ability to do these remarkable things. I could not have finished high school, with a full football scholarship and earn a college degree, without God on my side revealing key principles of success.

I experienced a broken femur at age seven, and later a broken foot. I wore a special shoe to correct and straighten my foot. I was hit by vehicles twice. One injury was serious; I was in hospital in traction for weeks. Told by doctors I would not be able to play football due to scoliosis; I also had trouble with reading and writing. With all the physical challenges, home dysfunction, and educational challenges I experienced, I still received good grades, become captain of the high school track team, was a state runner-up in the 400-meters in high school and run a 4.2 second forty-yard dash in college. These are pretty remarkable accomplishments. God wants to accomplish remarkable victories in our lives.

War with the prophecy spoken over your life through prayer, studying and fasting. We must position ourselves to receive remarkable secrets and that will unleash His manifestation of divine truths and victory. **1 Timothy 1:18 (NLT): "Timothy, my son hear my instruction for you, based on the prophetic words spoken about you earlier. May they help you fight well in the Lord's battle."**

We must go and take what God has promised! It will not just happen. You have to daily die to self and yield to the Holy Spirit's instruction.

Matthew 6:13: "And do not lead us into temptation, but deliver us from the evil one." We need the truth daily to deal with the lies that Satan throws at us.

1 Peter 5:8 (NLT) says: "Stay alert! Watch out for your great enemy, the devil. He prowls around like a roaring lion, looking for someone to devour." Satan is seeking to ambush us. We need God's insight of the enemy's schemes and tactics. I admit I have allowed the enemy to ambush me in seasons of my life as a young man. Sin takes you further than you ever planned and affects your future and those you have impacted by your poor choices. Sin leaves you broken, separated from God and embarrassed. Jesus is our redeemer and God wants us to stay close to His side, so we can see Satan's tactics and defeat Him with the power of the Holy Spirit and God's Holy Word.

Isaiah 55:9 (NLT) states: "For just as the heavens are higher than the earth, so my ways are higher than your ways and my thoughts higher than your thoughts." In our own understanding, we are limited, but we serve and know an unlimited God who wants us to succeed and be alert of our enemy's schemes. We as believers must be on the same frequency as the Lord, aligning our will with His.

A key scripture, **1 Corinthians 2:9-10 (NLT) states "No eye has seen, no ear has heard, and no mind has imagined what God has prepared for those who love him. But God hath revealed [them] unto us by his Spirit: for the Spirit searches all things, yea, and the deep things of God."** God has strategies to lead us to our destiny, but we must be still long enough to hear and receive what the

Holy Spirit is instructing. A life that is led by the Holy Spirit is a life that is a full of peace and adventure. Jesus said in **Matthew 11:28-30, "Come to Me, all you who labor and are heavy laden, and I will give you rest. Take my yoke upon you and learn from Me, I am gentle and lowly in heart, and you will find rest for your souls. For my yoke is easy and my burden is light."** It is exciting that God wants to show us secrets to the kingdom, which allows us to enjoy rest and peace in Him. When we are willing to receive the yoke of Christ, we accept the responsibility that the battle is the Lord's and we need to obey the leading of the Lord and follow God's Word and do what He says on a daily basis.

A yoke is a wooden bar or frame by which two draft animals are joined at the heads and neck for working together. When we take on Jesus' yoke, we can cooperate with the Holy Spirit to fulfill the wishes of God in our life and fulfill the plans of God as a team.

My father in the faith, Pastor Otis Lockett, Sr. once stated, "The greater the revelation, the greater the responsibility." When God reveals His will to us, we have a responsibility to obey God. The impartation helps us grow. When we share God's word it helps others grow.

In my times alone with God there is such awe and a Holy reverence that has helped me understand what we must do to advance His will to see souls come into the kingdom of God. Revelation is birthed in private prayer, a place of rest and of faith. God puts a fire in us that will compel us to impart what God is showing us to our family, friends, and people in our sphere of influence. Understand we are born for such a time as this! What God reveals to us to help redeem people to God and to advance His kingdom is important. The reason for this book is to help you gain insight about prayer that will help you and your family follow God in good, bad and ugly times of life, so God will receive the glory.

Elevating Moment:

The question is why do we need remarkable manifestations of truth? As I have cultivated a friendship with our God, the Father, I have come to learn God is the solution to our world's problems. He will entrust us with unusual secrets to provide solutions to our world's problems. He will give us vision in how we can help set people free from the bondage of Satan.

God revealed this strategy for reaching young people on a mountain in Black Mountain, NC in 1986. The three main points are an atmosphere of worship, excellent bible teaching, and exciting activities. I came to understand it is okay to have lots of fun as a Christian. As a young believer, I thought we did not want to disturb God or get too excited as a Christian. This was the mindset I learned by attending church and watching people who were religious. I wish I had been introduced to the word "enthusiasm" early in life. A characteristic of God is fullness of life and vitality.

I like **Ephesians 1:17: "That the God of our Lord Jesus Christ, the Father glory, may give unto you the spirit of wisdom and revelation in the knowledge of him."** God wants us to see who we are in Him; our identity is what we have inherited in Christ. For many seasons of my life, I walked around defeated, not understanding that I am a King's son. He loves me more than I realize. He wants you to know He has a bright future for you according to **Jeremiah 29:11:**

"'I know the plans [purpose] I have for you,' says the Lord, 'plans for good [completeness] and to give [entrust] you a future.'"

God values each of us so much that He has laid out a purpose that will bring peace and not destruction. He has entrusted us with a destiny that has a great outcome. Many of us have walked in defeat, believing the lies of the enemy. We must stop aligning our thoughts and minds with the lies from Satan. We must each align our life with what God says about us. If we sincerely ask God to reveal who we are in Him, He will bring tremendous breakthrough for us through the power of the Holy Spirit.

Prayer Elevating Moment

Pray this prayer if you have struggled with aligning with God's agenda. "Lord, bring my heart and mind into alignment with your purposes for my life. I give up what is not aligned to you Jesus. I choose, as an act of my will, to turn away from lies of the enemy in Jesus' name."

John 17:21, "Help me become one with you Jesus as you and the Father and the Holy Spirit are one." I admit, I have struggled for many years with rejection, insecurity and forgetting who I am in Christ. I have to remind myself repeatedly of who I am in Christ. We must deal with the past, but not focus on the past. Our focus must be on Jesus and the Word. Making a regular confession of what the Word of God says about us is vital.

For example: I will confess aloud, "I am Rex, God's servant. I am more than a conqueror, and I am deeply loved by God." Reading and speaking the Word out loud helps you know your identity. Hearing how God feels and sees you is life-changing and transforming! We live in a world where Satan and his cohorts try to make us feel like we are of no worth. You must decide and know in your heart and mind that you are loved and important to God.

Know you are God's son or daughter and this involves having a greater sense of purpose and destiny. Knowing purpose brings completeness and wholeness; you are God's valuable jewel and the Spirit of God is alive in you. When we know our value, we have the ability to cooperate with God to do remarkable things that leave a legacy of blessings for generations. **Daniel 11:32: "But they that know their God shall be strong and do great exploits."**

Experiencing Elevated Remarkability
Review

1. What does the Hebrew word *chazon* mean? Why do we need it?

2. How can we align with God's ways?

3. Why do we need to understand our identity in Christ?

4. How do you know you are valuable to God?

5. What is God's phone number?

6. How do we align our thoughts with God's plan?

7. Why is confessing the word vital to the Christ follower?

What testimony has encouraged you?

_____

_____

_____

_____

Suggested Reading:

Ephesians 1

1 Peter 5

Jeremiah 33

Matthew 11

A remarkable revelation comes when we understand the necessity of rest.

Hebrews 4:10-11: "For all who entered into God's rest have rested from their labors, just as God did after creating the world. So let us do our best to enter that rest. But if we disobey God, as the people of Israel did, we will fail." I have spent too many seasons of my life striving to do God's work, thinking I had to work relentless hours to accomplish God's work.

Do we think we are greater than God? Working continuously, not taking time to rest, relax or reflect? We must take time to stop and allow our bodies and minds the time to refresh and recharge. I believe many health challenges are the result of a lack of rest. This can and will lead to a premature departure from earth. Pastor Garvin, an administrative pastor in Colorado Springs, stated, "The rest of God is like the fragrance of heaven; it draws creation and draws people." We must discipline ourselves to take time to refresh to be effective servants of God.

When we learn to be still and rest in God, His Word exposes our true heart and motives. We cannot dismiss ungodly thoughts as though they are not in our heart. Being still helps us deal with our heart and allows the Holy Spirit to bring light to wrong thoughts and motives. We then can renounce the thoughts that Satan tries to plant in our heart, so they will not take root. Let's be honest: when we are exhausted, we are more vulnerable to get into the flesh, thinking ungodly thoughts, speaking ungodly words and participating in ungodly habits. This is exactly why it's vital that we rest and be still before God on a consistent basis.

We must allow the Holy Spirit to show us what is going on in us, so we can be in proper alignment with the Father. People don't fall into sin all of a sudden. It is a process of running past the internal alerts of the Holy Spirit and the wise counsel of leaders. When we are too busy to stop to be alone with God, we are in danger of being ambushed by Satan. When we don't take regular showers in the word, we can stink up our homes with our attitudes and our work places become polluted with words that are not of a Christ follower.

Hebrews 4:13: "And there is no creature hidden from His sight, but all things are naked and open to the eyes of Him to whom we must give account." God can see all of our thoughts, motives and desires. We will have to give account to God! It is better to settle up with the Lord on a daily basis than to cause destruction week after week and then reflect to see years of doing things our way and the harm and destruction we have caused our families and friends.

Hebrews 4:15: "For we do not have a High Priest who cannot sympathize with our weaknesses, but was in all points tempted as we are, yet without sin." Jesus knows what it feels like to walk in this flesh suit. He knows how our mind works and desires to fulfill the fleshly cravings. Remember, the Spirit has more power than the flesh. The key to success is being plugged into the power source of the Holy Spirit. In order for a lamp to have light, it must be plugged into a power source. My power equation is: prayer + praise + rest = power.

According to Psalm 16:11, "You will show me the path of life; in Your presence is fullness of joy; At Your right hand are pleasures forevermore." God shows us the right way to go in life and the benefits are joy and pleasures forever. There are pleasures in God that are out of this world and can be only understood by the Holy Spirit.

Prayer Elevating Moment:

1. Lord, grant us vision.

2. Help me achieve victory in every area of my life.

3. Help me to reach out beyond myself and move out of my comfort zone.

4. Help me be willing to share with others what you are revealing to me.

5. Help me to let go, willingly submitting to your stretching of my faith.

6. Help me understand your purpose for my life.

7. To give heed to your constant call.

Source: "Prayers for every day." **James 1:5-6 states, "If any you lack wisdom, let him ask of God, who gives to all liberally and without reproach and it will** be given him. But let him ask in faith, with no doubting, for he who doubts is like the wave of the sea driven and tossed by the wind." When you don't know something, ask God for guidance and believe He will reveal His will to you. What God reveals will not make natural sense, but we must trust Him.

Proverbs 3:5 states, "Trust in the Lord with all your heart and lean not to your own understanding." The word "trust" in Greek is *batach*, meaning, "be bold or secure." Be secure in knowing God's heart and knowledge of His will for your life. God has given us faculties in accordance with the Word that help us choose practical steps of wisdom.

1 Thessalonians 5:20-21 (AMP): "But test and prove all things until you recognize what is good to, hold fast." We need discernment from the Holy Spirit in how to remain victorious in this walk of faith. Simply recognized, there is an enemy who hates us and looks for ways to destroy us. The word tells us that Satan comes to kill, steal and destroy (John 8:44). I believe when we walk with God on a daily basis, we have divine protection. That is not to say our lives will be absent of problems and trials. Jesus said, "In the world you will have trouble but be of good cheer I have overcome the world" (John 6:44). I can look back at seasons of my life and see how God kept me from certain destructive decisions that could have caused shame, hurt and a premature death. Our daily walk with God gives preservation from destructive temptations.

Prayer Elevating Moments

Lord, if I am living in ignorance of the truth by thinking things that are not aligned with your Word, please reveal areas I need to change. Help me be aware of any decision that I need to be making. I ask you to reveal that to me now in Jesus' name, amen.

Elevating Moment

Meeting my wife came through Balinda Deitz, who walked through her living room one fall day in 1986 and heard the Lord say to her, "Introduce Rex and Vickie to each other." Her plan was to prepare a picnic lunch for four at Optimist Park in Hickory, NC. We now have called that lunch the "love hoagies lunch" because it did not take long for me to realize I loved Vickie.

I vividly remember that fall day with the smell of flowers and the anticipation of another great football season. The lunch prepared tasted heavenly and Vickie looked a like a gorgeous angel wearing a dress and her hair so perfectly fixed. Ten months later, I married Vickie. The amazing part of all this was we had the blessings of our pastors and my college football coach. Getting married while I was still in college is not the normal route to take in a relationship, but God amazingly provided for us. God continues to do remarkable things now!

Another remarkable moment was when I was clearly called to ministry. One evening while in a Bible study, a word came forth about a calling on my life, then not long from that time a guest evangelist confirmed again my call to preach. We were in service at Christian ministry fellowship where Pastor Ralph and Hilda Britain were pastors. The prophetic word stated, "There is a greater degree of cooperation that you can begin to add to your life. There is a calling there. It will take week's months until you are in the fulfillment of this thing. But, it will require the cutting of lines to get where God wants you to be. An inner yielding is what it will require." I see this word being fulfilled when we moved to Colorado. In 1991, when I did my trial sermon, Pastor Otis Lockett Sr. stated, "I know Rex is called." I still remember his remarkable words to this day.

Experiencing Elevated Remarkability
Review

1. Why should rest be a priority for the believer?

2. How do we receive power?

3. Why should we be of good cheer according to John 6:44?

4. How should we handle trouble?

5. How can we put our trust in God?

Are you taking time to stop and rest?

_____

_____

_____

_____

Suggested Reading:

Hebrews 4

James 1

Proverbs 3

1 Thessalonians 5

Step Three: Authority

1 Timothy 2:1-3

Therefore I exhort first of all that supplications, prayers, intercession, and giving of thanks be made for all men, for kings and all who are in authority, that we may lead quiet and peaceable life in all godliness and reverence. This is good and acceptable in the sight of God our Savior, who desires all men to be saved and come to the knowledge of the truth.

In step three, I believe every person wants to experience peace and quiet marked by godliness. To enjoy and experience peace, we must pray for those in leadership roles, so they will protect laws that promote good in the land and not laws that promote evil. God's Word is our guide for ruling government. George Washington once said, "It is impossible to govern rightly without God and the Bible." When we do not like a leader's behavior or policies, it does not exempt the Christ follower from praying for leaders. All believers are called by God to pray for those in positions of authority. We also have a responsibility to be engaged in segments of society that influence culture. Don't complain about our world when you are not willing to do something about it.

"Authority" means one invested with power. In the Greek, "authority" is *exousia* meaning "the power of choice." When our life is in line with God's Word, we have a choice in the outcome of a circumstance. If we understood the authority we have in Christ, we would definitely utilize that power and authority that has been given to the followers of Christ. Satan attempts to keep us in the dark concerning the authority we have in Jesus' name. I believe if we ask God to reveal our authority in Him, we would be amazed. Jesus said to the centurion in Luke 7:2-9 (NLT):

> **At that time the highly valued slave of a roman officer was sick and near death. When the officer heard Jesus, he sent some respected Jewish elders to ask him to come and heal his slave. So they earnestly begged Jesus to help the man. "If anyone deserves your help, he does," they said, "for he loves the Jewish people and even built a synagogue for us." So Jesus went with them. But just before they arrived at the house, the officer sent some friends to say, "Lord, don't trouble yourself by coming to my home, I am not worthy of such honor. I am not even worthy to come and meet you. Just say the word from where you are, and my servant will be healed. I know this because I am under authority of my superior officers, and I have authority over my soldiers. I only need to say, 'Go and they go, or Come and they come.' And if I say to my slaves, 'Do this, they do it.'" When**

Jesus heard this, he was amazed. Turning to the crowd that was following him, he said, "I tell you, I haven't seen faith like this in all Israel!"

When we are under authority of the Word, meaning our life is governed by the Word of God, we recognize the humility we must walk in. Then we have the ability to use the authority invested to us by God. The problem with many leaders is they are not under the authority of the Word of God; therefore, they have no power to defeat the enemy.

We are to be strong in the Lord and in the power of His might. The first area we must take authority over is our mouth. We must not forget to align our heart and mouth with God's Word.

The second area is our thought life. Scripture tells us in Proverbs 23:7, **"For as a he thinks in his heart so is he."** We become and carry out the things we think about. Satan tries to get us to buy into thoughts and if we believe Satan's lies, he gains access to the ground of our thinking which eventually become actions.

2 Corinthians 10:3-6 (NLT):

We are human, but we don't wage war as humans do. We use God's mighty weapons, not worldly weapons, to knock down the strongholds of human reasoning and to destroy false arguments. We destroy every proud obstacle that keeps people from knowing God. We capture their rebellious thoughts and teach

them to obey Christ. And after you have become fully obedient,

we will punish everyone who remains disobedient.

We must use our authority in our personal life first. We must understand and realize we are in a war! We must be prepared for war.

Proverbs 4:24 says, "guard your heart above all else for out of it are the issues of life." When we speak God's Word, it is a powerful tool of defeating our enemies! **Hebrews 4:12 (NLT) states, "For the word of God is alive and powerful. It is sharper than the sharpest two-edged sword, cutting between soul and spirit, between joint and marrow. It exposes our innermost thoughts and desires."**

Ephesians 6:10-18 (NLT):

A final word: Be strong in the Lord and in his mighty power. Put on all of God's armor so that you will be able to stand firm against all strategies of the devil. For we are not fighting against flesh-and-blood enemies, but against evil rulers and authorities of the unseen world, against mighty powers in this dark world, and against evil spirits in the heavenly places. Therefore, put on every piece of God's armor so you will be able to resist the enemy in the time of evil. Then after the battle you will still be standing firm. Stand your ground, putting on the belt of truth and the body armor of God's righteousness for shoes, put on the peace that comes from the Good News so that you will be

fully prepared in addition to all of these, hold up the shield of faith to stop the fiery arrows of the devil. Put on salvation as your helmet, and take the sword of the Spirit, which is the word of God. Pray in the Spirit at all times and on every occasion. Stay alert and be persistent in your prayers for all believers everywhere.

We must put on the armor of God as an act of faith as we engage in a battle that cannot be seen with the natural eye. When we practice putting on the armor daily with our confession, we send a signal to the Kingdom of heaven and the kingdom of darkness that we are fully prepared for battle dressed in Jesus Christ our victor and protector. When we are prepared in prayer, dressed for battle, God can call us into action more rapidly to war and gain victory for the Kingdom.

Hebrews 12:1-2 (NLT):

Therefore, since we are surrounded by such a huge crowd of witnesses to the life of faith, let us strip off every weight that slows us down, especially the sin that so easily trips us up. And let us run with endurance the race God has set before us. We do this by keeping our eyes on Jesus, the champion who initiates and perfects our faith. Because of the joy awaiting him, he endured the cross, disregarding its shame. Now he is seated in the place of honor beside God's throne.

Just as at a football game, we cheer on our favorite team knowing the players can compete because they are properly dressed for the game, the same applies for our spiritual battle. When we are properly prepared for battle, we can be successful in our fight of faith. Our speech mixed with faith and God's Word is the key to aligning with God's kingdom agenda and authority. **Isaiah 55:11:**

> **So shall My word be that goes forth my mouth; It shall not return unto Me void, But it shall accomplish what I please, And it shall prosper in the thing which I sent it. When we say what God's word says in accordance to his will and divine timing heaven will act on our behalf.**

Luke 10:19: "Behold, I give you the authority to trample on serpents and scorpions, and over all the power of the enemy, and nothing by any means shall hurt you." Jesus has given us power to defeat our enemy; we have to appropriate this authority and make sure Satan is not attacking us by some legal right we have made with our own words, thoughts and actions.

2 Timothy 4:18: "And the Lord will deliver me from every evil work and preserve me for His heavenly kingdom. To Him be glory forever and ever. Amen!"

I remember when I was a youth pastor in the 90's, one of our young people was hit by a car. This young man was in a coma. The amazing thing about this story is when I entered the hospital room to visit him, the young man's mother stated, "Pastor Rex is here." He immediately came out of the coma. I was definitely surprised and humbled by this move of God. He made a full recovery!

Elevating Moment:

To every Christ follower, Jesus is our Lord and Savior. Jesus has given us power and authority. It is our choice whether we appropriate that authority. We have the authority in Christ Jesus to bind Satan. What exactly does the word bind mean? To confine, restrict and restrain. We, by the authority in Christ, confine the enemy in Jesus' name. Christ ratifies what is done in His name and in obedience to His Word on earth. To ratify means to give formal consent or agreement making it officially valid. **Matthew 16:19: "And I will give you the keys of the kingdom of heaven, and whatever you bind on earth will be bound in heaven, and whatever you loose on earth will be loosed in heaven."** When we understand and submit ourselves to God's Word, God promises He will give us keys to righteousness, peace and joy in the Holy Spirit.

Elevating Moment:

Colorado has a lot of hiking trails. My friend Gary and I went for a hike near the Monument area capturing spectacular views from every direction. We had started our prayer journey and saw a biker coming toward us. He warned us a storm was coming and we noticed a few sprinkles of rain began to fall. We stopped and discussed if we should head back. I said, "We've come this far—why not keep going?"

Gary was hesitant about proceeding due to the heavy clouds and light rain, which could turn into heavy rain at any moment. Then Gary spoke to the storm to go north in Jesus' name. In amazement, I witnessed with my own eyes the storm change directions and head north. We were able to enjoy the journey for the rest of the evening with no rain. Talk about appropriating authority in the earth, Gary demonstrated what Jesus did on the Sea of Galilee rebuking the storms.

Jesus releases from heaven the authority of His Word into the earth. Therefore, when we align with God's agenda and speak His Word in accordance to God's agenda, we will see results from our prayers. When we truly understand who we are in Jesus, we will not walk around defeated, depressed or oppressed. I admit, on many occasions I have forgotten who I am in Christ. Satan tries to make us forget who we are in times of temptations. When we remain in God's Word, we can clearly recognize the subtleties of the enemy. We must be steadfast and intentional and schedule regular times with the Lord, using His authority to bind Satan from his operations in our homes, communities, cities, nation and world.

Elevating Moment:

I recently received a phone call from my cousin. He updated his phone to make sure my number was a working number. He began to share with me how God has blessed him, taking me back in time to a season in his life that was dark. He told me he had made many wrong decisions and was strung out on drugs. He said his mother called me to come and pray for him. When I arrived at their home, I began to anoint the entire house with anointing oil, and then he said I asked him if he wanted to be free. He said yes. He told me he remembers I took the anointing oil and laid hands on the back of his head while he was on the floor. My cousin said demons began to leave him from his mouth and he screamed from the core of his being, "I am *free,* I am *free.*" God's Word tells us **John 8:36 (NLT), "So if the Son sets you free, you are truly free."**

He then told me this was the first time he realized God is real! He acknowledges he had a touch of God on his life the day I prayed for him. My cousin now has a successful business and a family. He said only God could turn a person's life around and the turning point for him was when I anointed him. To God be the glory because I obviously had forgotten about that time. I have heard similar stories from individuals over the years and I know it is God who works through the person of the Holy Spirit.

Elevating Moment:

Vickie and I attended leadership training in Estes Park on September 21, 2014. This was with Cityconexx, a ministry based in Denver, CO. We enjoyed the outdoor weather on park benches. One of the leaders received a call from his father that he had to make an emergency trip home from Kansas to Indiana and requested prayer. Dean prayed and the Holy Spirit prompted me to pray. I asked if I could pray. I prayed for the situation and as soon as I said, "in Jesus' name," a clap of thunder happened with no storms or cloud around. This was another amazing wonder. I believe angels were dispatched to handle the matter.

John 12:28-29: "Father, glorify Your name. Then a voice came from heaven, saying, 'I have both glorified it and will glorify it again.; Therefore the people who stood by and heard it said that it had thundered. Others said, 'An angel has spoken to Him.'" When we understand the authority that has been given to us, I believe we are more careful in our actions and will walk with humility.

Prayer Elevating Moment

Lord, help me see and understand my authority as a believer and Jesus, help me to abide with you daily. I ask you, Holy Spirit, to open my eyes to show me how to walk in authority. Show me how to grow in my authority. Help me make wise choices that elevate my family, friends and future.

Acts 4:29-31, Revelation 2:26

Experiencing Elevated Authority
Review

1. With whom is our fight, according to 2 Corinthians 10:3-6?

2. How can we fight a spiritual battle, according to Hebrews 4:12?

3. Why do we need God's armor, according to Ephesians 6:10-14?

4. What does the Word in Luke 10:19 mean by "trample on serpents and scorpions"?

5. Why does God's Word tell believers to guard their heart (Proverbs 4:24)?

6. What is authority?

7. Why was Jesus amazed by the centurion's faith?

What battle are you facing today?

_____

_____

_____

_____

Suggested Reading:

1 Timothy 2

2 Corinthians 10

Ephesians 6

Luke 10

Step Four: Yield

Isaiah 1:19: "If ye be willing and obedient,

ye shall eat the good of the land."

Step four is when we learn to yield to God in every area of our lives, we will experience divine victories simply because we will be in places where God wants us to be to enforce His authority and plan. When we are where God leads us, there are opportunities to bring salvation to a lost and dying world!

Yield means to give. We must surrender of our will and become obedient to the leading of the Holy Spirit. We must merge our will with God's will. To be effective for the Kingdom of God, we have to have a greater cooperation with the Lord. We must develop our inner hearing so we can receive precise instructions from the Lord.

Isaiah 1:19 says, "If ye be willing and obedient, ye shall eat the good of the land." The key word is "willing." We must adjust our mind and will to be ready to obey the Lord's instruction daily. Remember, there are ramifications for disobeying clear instructions from the Lord. **1 Samuel 13:13: "'How foolish!'**

Samuel exclaimed. **'You have not kept the command the Lord your God gave you. Had you kept it, the Lord would have established your kingdom over Israel.'"** I have discovered life is more fulfilling when we yield to God's specific instructions. God knows all things including what is best for our life. Yielding to God puts us in a place to advance God's kingdom. In essence, we must decide to allow the Holy Spirit to guide and manage our daily living with inner promptings.

Memorization and meditation of Isaiah 1:19 broke the mindset of always wanting to do things my way instead of what God lead and instructed for me. I remember looking in the mirror as a young college student telling myself, "If you, Rex, be willing and obedient, you shall eat the good of the land." I personalized the scripture in my life.

Mark 16:15 (**NLT**) gives us a clear mandate from Jesus, the King of kings: **"and then he told them, 'Go into all the world and preach the Good News to everyone.'"** If we truly and fully understand we belong to Christ, we would yield more to God. Oftentimes, we allow fear or circumstances to control our decisions. I remember when God spoke to me about becoming His minister. I was hesitant because I looked at my lack of training and abilities. I did not feel qualified to be called into ministry, but who God calls, He qualifies.

1 Corinthians 6:19 (NLT): "Don't you realize that your body is the temple of the Holy Spirit, who lives in you and was given to you by God?" You do not belong to yourself.

1 Corinthians 6:20 (NLT): "for God bought you with a high price. So you must honor God with your body." It is imperative we cooperate with the Holy Spirit; this particular verse explains why we must yield. **Romans 10:14-15 (NLT):**

But how can they call on him to save them unless they believe in him? And how can they believe in him if they have never heard about him? And how can they hear about him unless someone tells them? And how will anyone go and tell them without being sent? That is why the Scriptures say, "How beautiful are the feet of messengers who bring good news!"

While we move forward in the commission, we also must pray that fellow believers follow the mandate given by Jesus. How many reading this book have received specific instructions from the Lord to do something? If you have not acted on God's instruction, I want to encourage you to do so, for it is not about you, but about bringing people into knowledge of Jesus Christ. I am reminded of a family we visited while in Florida. This daughter told me when her father was in the hospital battling cancer that her father said, "I can't die now; there are many things that God told me to do." This father came to a realization of how precious time is and obedience to what God tells us. This father passed away a few days later. He secured his heavenly home, but realized before passing that he did not fulfill his purpose in his lifetime. Case and point: while you have life in you, do all God tells you to do and leave the results to Him. God wants us to believe Him and obey.

Elevating Moment

Answering the call from God to serve as the Colorado National Day of Prayer Coordinator this past January, in the spring of 2014, I had my prayer time and I heard the Lord say to me, "Go to Denver."

I asked, "What for?" I did not get a specific reason, but I went to Denver and upon arrival, I felt lead to go by the state capitol. I parked my car and climbed to the top of the capital steps facing south and prayed a short prayer. Then I went back home. The next day I received word that the governor's proclamation arrived earlier than it ever has. Typically, the office would receive the proclamation one day before the National Day of Prayer event held every first Thursday in May. God wants our obedience; leave the results to God.

Luke 10:2 (NLT) says, "These were his instructions to them: 'The harvest is great, but the workers are few. So pray to the Lord who is in charge of the harvest; ask him to send more workers into his fields.'" We must yield completely to God in order to be used completely by God.

In 1995, I began to sense change was coming. I had served as Executive Director of Malachi House, a home for men with life-controlling issues. During this assignment, prayer was a means of survival, because I dealt with men whose way of life was typical of lying, stealing and manipulating to get their wants satisfied. Quality time with God was essential to have discernment handling men who were accustomed to lying and manipulating.

One particular evening I secured the church as groups finished up Bible studies. When I arrived, all the groups were already finished. I went into the sanctuary to pray and from the bottom of my heart in a cry of desperation, I said to God, **"Show me what to do so that I can do it!"**

I heard a voice in my spirit, say, "Colorado."

I was surprised and said, "Lord, if this is you, please confirm this instruction."

I received undeniable confirmations that God had spoken to me. I knew I must yield to God. Remember, when you decide to follow God's plan, there will come other opportunities that distract you from yielding to God. I enjoyed serving on staff in North Carolina and that season ended, but another opportunity was presented to me in North Carolina. I was so excited that I told Vickie I wanted to take this new opportunity. Vickie asked me, "What about Colorado?"

I said, "I know, but I want to do this now."

Listen very closely. I need to share an important insight with you. When God says, "Behold," or, "Look," you need to pay close attention to what God is saying to you. For the first time in my walk with God, I experienced the holy fear of God and realized I did not have an option if I wanted all of God's best for my life. I became afraid of jeopardizing the protection of my family and His best for us. This was a reverential fear, knowing God is serious about obedience and aligning with His plan.

At that particular season of my life, I was a part-time bus driver. I arrived early at the school and waited for school to be released. I read my Bible and books about leadership. On that particular day in the spring of 1996, I felt impressed to read **Exodus 23:20-22, 25:**

> **Behold, I send an angel before you to keep you in the way and to bring you into a place which I have prepared. Beware of Him and obey His voice; do not provoke Him, for He will not pardon your transgression; for My name is in Him. But if you indeed obey His voice and do all that I speak, then I will be enemy to**

**your enemies and an adversary to your adversaries. For my
angel will go before you and bring you in.**

This act of obedience has led to hundreds of people coming into God's kingdom. The Lord has done exceedingly abundantly above all I could ever ask or think. It's amazing how many souls have come to Christ and how many have been discipled through our obedience. I have developed friends that have enhanced my life as a leader. I also have been afforded opportunities far beyond my comprehension. Following God's ways is an adventure and can be challenging. The fulfillment of seeing lives touched for the glory of God is awesome and amazing. I challenge all who are reading this book to yield your life completely to God so you can be aligned to make a greater impact for God's kingdom business!

Fathers, mothers, sons and daughters, we all must yield to God in how He wants us to govern our homes. A home full of strife and anger gives Satan a foothold in the lives of our family members. Strife and selfish ambition open the door to Satan for every evil work. This is a rude reality. Husband and wife must find a way to bring Christ to the center by dealing with life problems and issues in a Christ-like way. I regret to say we have had many seasons in our home where we have not elevated above the strife and it helps us see clearly how Satan is trying to operate against us by not always being in peace, loving and willing to yield to God. Being a believer means dying to self and allowing Christ to increase as we decrease (John 3:30).

Yes, I know it is easier said than practiced. God said work out your salvation with fear and trembling. When we partake in prayer, power is produced to set captives free. For the sake of our children, as well as to honor God, we must yield to God and elevate prayer in our homes.

James 3:17: "But the wisdom from above is first of all pure. It is also peace loving, gentle at all times and willing to yield to others, full of mercy and good deeds. It shows no favoritism and is always sincere." In order to live a life yielded to God we must spend time with God daily so we can be filled with His Spirit. This text clearly tells us how the atmosphere of environments should look and sound. Too often, we become so busy with work and life that we are empty spiritually. Stop a moment and let God fill you up right now with His Holy Spirit.

Prayer Elevating Moment

Lord, give me the ability to yield to your leading more and more throughout my life. Lord, you know where is the safest place and best for me. In your Word, you said, "He who loses his life for my sake will find it and he who protects his life will lose it." Help me let go and let you live fully through me, for you must increase and I must decrease.

I have not always yielded to God, and in the times I didn't, I have learned tough lessons of a life of disobedience. I have discovered yielding to God is much better than things my way.

Disobedience demotes.

I knew God led me to attend Lenoir Rhyne University, I chose Western Carolina University because it was bigger, more popular in the mid-eighties and the head coach Bob Waters visited my high school. I was impressed and flattered that coach Bob Waters specifically came to visit me and asked me to come to

Western Carolina University in 1984. I chose this path despite the leading from the Lord to attend Lenoir Rhyne University. The first semester of college was a disaster academically, with only one credit hour and a broken wrist, which ended my football season in 1984. When things don't work out, we tend to get mad at God and blame Him for the outcome. **Proverbs 19:3 (NLT): "People ruin their lives by their own foolishness and then are angry at the Lord."**

We must remember, when we choose our own way, we must take full responsibility for our choices especially when we don't consult God first. I also became alarmed I could not sense God's presence or hear His voice. My disobedience caused my spiritual life to suffer. Church attendance was not a priority; the only thing kept intact was my daily Bible reading. God did not overrule my will to go to Western Carolina University, but the experience taught me a valuable lesson. To obey God's direction, and where He is leading, is a life that is much more fulfilling. Remember, our obedience to God positions us to be connected to people who help us fulfill God's purpose and destiny for our lives. Obedience advances God's kingdom; that is why we must cooperate with the Holy Spirit's leading. However, the amazing thing about our Lord is He can use our mistakes to bring glory to Him. He is sovereign and in control.

Another time I missed God was when I had a long delay in gaining employment, simply because I made the assumption God wanted us to live in a specific city, without first asking the Lord. We then realized God sent us near my hometown. One must remember, wherever God sends you, there are times you will face challenges. Since I knew God sent us to a new area, I had no idea of the hardships I would face as a young supervisor. God gives us the grace to handle difficult times.

Hebrew 10:36 states, **"You have need of endurance after you have done the will of God you will receive the promise."** This particular scripture was a verse I meditated on for nearly three years. I had to align and yield my will into God's will. This was difficult because since my early childhood, I was used to doing whatever I wanted to do. I was accustomed to running the streets late at night, skipping school and being defiant to authority. God used this season of my life to forge discipline and submission into my life. When I finally accepted His will, I heard God say, "You are now ready for the promise or next assignment." I wish I had been more cooperative sooner, not resisting the trials and tribulations I had faced as a young distribution supervisor in Burlington, NC. I am reminded of the word I received, **"There is a greater degree of cooperation that you can begin to add to your life."**

Experiencing Elevated Yield

Review

1. Why do we need to obey God? (Isaiah 1:19)

2. What mandate do we have from Jesus? (Mark 16:15)

3. What is significant in Exodus 23:20-22 for the Tonkins moving to Colorado?

4. What demotes your life?

5. What kind of wisdom comes from above?

6. What is significant about the word "behold"?

Has God instructed you to do something?

_____

_____

_____

_____

Suggested Reading:

Isaiah 1

Mark 16

1 Corinthians 6

Romans 10

Step Five: Empower

Ephesians 3:16 (NLT)

"I pray that from his glorious, unlimited resources he will empower you with inner strength through his Spirit."

I understand it is Jesus who has empowered me to graduate from high school, college and to be a minister of the gospel.

The word, "empower" means to equip with power and ability. As we seek the Lord and draw near to Him, God will draw near to us. The word "proximity" means near. Proximity to power translates to empowerment. When we are close to God in prayer, we become empowered. **Ephesians 3:16-20 (NLT):**

> **I pray that from his glorious, unlimited resources he will empower you with inner strength through his Spirit. Then Christ will make his home in your hearts as you trust in him. Your roots will grow down into God's love and keep you strong.**

And may you have the power to understand, as all God's people should, how wide, how long, how high, and how deep his love is. May you experience the love of Christ, though it is too great to understand fully. Then you will be made complete with all the fullness of life and power that comes from God. Now all glory to God, who is able, through his mighty power at work within us, to accomplish infinitely more than we might ask or think.

1 Chronicles 16:11 (NLT): "Search for the LORD and for his strength."

When we develop a daily discipline to seek God we will have daily supply and strength to face each day. God's Word says we will receive power (*dynamis* in Greek means strength, power and ability). This *dynamis* is the same power that raised Jesus from the dead. It also means moral power and excellence of soul. As Christ followers, we must become desperate to grab hold of all God intends for us to have. In a culture where we see moral failure in every sphere of influence, we need the power of the Holy Spirit working in our lives. One question that often comes up in Christian circles regards that of the Holy Spirit. Because the Holy Spirit is so effective in working in our lives, Satan often fights the person of the Holy Spirit. Many try to rationalize receiving from the Holy Spirit because they lack understanding aspects of the gifts of the Spirit, signs and wonders.

Jesus stated in **Acts 1:8 (NLT): "But you will receive power when the Holy Spirit comes upon you. And you will be my witnesses, telling people about me**

everywhere in Jerusalem, throughout Judea, in Samaria, and to the ends of the earth." The Holy Spirit comes alongside believers to empower us for service.

I love the story of Jackie Robinson. When he was on the brink of total defeat and despair due to racial prejudice, one of his fellow teammates came alongside him to support him and empower him. The significance of this story is Jackie Robinson suffered much persecution as the first black man to play for a professional baseball team. He was called degrading names by many fans. His teammate, who was white, stood with him in the midst of pain and rejection. His teammate helped bring peace and affirmation. This course of action is a clear example of how the Holy Spirit comes alongside us when Satan constantly ridicules and condemns us. This decision by Jackie's teammate changed the destiny of Jackie's career in baseball.

When we feel like it is the end of the road, the Holy Spirit guides us into truth of what God has in store for us. **Colossians 3:13 and Ephesians 4:2 say, "Bear one another's burdens."** The Greek word *anechomai* means, "to sustain, bear, or hold up against a thing, come alongside." The second word *bastaxo* means, "to lift, or carry something with the idea to carry it away or remove." Jackie's teammate helped carry away a mindset that almost destroyed Jackie. Today number 42, which was Jackie's number, is displayed in every major league baseball field in recognition of the difference he made. The Holy Spirit will help us through life's tough spots so we can live victoriously.

When thought patterns contradict God's word, the Holy Spirit gently reveals this attitude so that we can walk in truth. In **John 20:21-22, it states, "So Jesus said to them again, 'Peace to you! As the Father has sent Me so I send you.'**

And when He had said this He breathed on them and said, 'Receive ye the Holy Spirit.'" Jesus knew when servants are sent out they will need to be endued with power and Jesus breathed on them and said, "Receive the Holy Spirit." The sad part about the Christian is we have a form of godliness, but deny the power of the Holy Spirit. Let none of us quench or grieve the Holy Spirit, but grab hold of all God intends for us to have.

Genesis 32:28: "Jacob said, 'I will not let thee go, except thou bless me.'" We must wrestle in prayer, with the Lord, thirsting and hungering with all that is within us for more of God. We must be real with God and covet the gifts of the Spirit until we obtain new understanding and power that is in God. In the sport of wrestling, the strength is in the neck, chest, and thigh; the thigh is the strength of all. So God touched Jacob's thigh; with that strength in his thigh gone, defeat is imminent. What did Jacob do? He hung on (Smith Wigglesworth, 97). When we lay hold of God and receive God's best for our lives, we gain strength to face our greatest fear. For Jacob, his fear was his brother Esau. Jacob took his birthright of inheritance. When we truly want and receive God's power, we gain the ability to walk in victory and see God restore relationships.

Prayer Elevating Moments:

Lord, I may not understand everything about your Word, but you said the Holy Spirit will guide us into all truth. Therefore Lord, I choose to receive all you desire me to have, help me to hunger for more of you Lord and your Word.

In **Acts 12:5-17** we see the effective fervent prayer of saints praying for the apostle Peter empowered him to continue the work of the cross. **"But while Peter**

was in prison, the church prayed very earnestly for him." Earnest means, in Greek, stretch out the hand with intense prayer. This describes the prayer made for Peter, and he was delivered from prison.

> **The night before Peter was to be placed on trial, he was asleep, fastened with two chains between two soldiers. Others stood guard at the prison gate. Suddenly, there was a bright light in the cell, and an angel of the Lord stood before Peter. The angel struck him on the side to awaken him and said, "Quick! Get up!" And the chains fell off his wrists. Then the angel told him, "Get dressed and put on your sandals." And he did. "Now put on your coat and follow me," the angel ordered.**

Peter experienced instant empowerment because of the constant prayers made on his behalf. We can clearly see why intercessors make the difference when it comes to gaining freedom and victory to advance God's work.

> **So Peter left the cell, following the angel. But all the time he thought it was a vision. He didn't realize it was actually happening. They passed the first and second guard posts and came to the Iron Gate leading to the city, and this opened for them all by itself. So they passed through and started walking down the street, and then the angel suddenly left him. Peter finally came to his senses.**

"It's really true!" he said. "The Lord has sent his angel and saved me from Herod and from what the Jewish leaders had planned to do to me!"

When he realized this, he went to the home of Mary, the mother of John Mark, where many were gathered for prayer. He knocked at the door in the gate, and a servant girl named Rhoda came to open it. When she recognized Peter's voice, she was so overjoyed that, instead of opening the door, she ran back inside and told everyone, "Peter is standing at the door!"

"You're out of your mind!" they said.

When she insisted, they decided, "It must be his angel."

Meanwhile, Peter continued knocking. When they finally opened the door and saw him, they were amazed. He motioned for them to quiet down and told them how the Lord had led him out of prison. "Tell James and the other brothers what happened," he said. And then he went to another place.

This particular text should be a reminder to each of us to keep on praying and not give up on things where we need a breakthrough. When God answers our prayers, why are we amazed when He answers?

Elevating Moments:

I remember many years ago Vickie was awakened from a sound sleep and sat straight up in bed. She saw a vision of fire and sensed her brother Ricky was in danger. Ricky was in the Army and because of the secrecy of his assignments we rarely knew where he was stationed. Cindy Jacobs, in her book *Possessing The Gates,* calls this, "prophetic intercession." Vickie remained in prayer until she had gotten a release in prayer. The next time we saw Ricky was at his home in Clarksville, TN. He told us a situation where the barracks they lived in was bombed and miraculously all the troops in his company survived. This documented attack happened in Germany and Vickie believes all the troops survived because of prayer.

I believe God wants to warn us, but we sometimes are so busy with life to stop. Remember when someone comes to your mind, pray for that person. Two other amazing stories are when a little boy felt President Reagan was in danger. The little boy complained of his tummy hurting. The mother was right on target in sensing the need to pray for the president. Unbeknownst to this family, there was an assassination attempt on President Ronald Reagan. What would have happened if they had not paused to pray for the President? Once they felt a release, the boy's tummy stop hurting. The story has more details in Cindy Jacob's book, *Possessing The Gates.*

One other story is about Shirley Dobson sensing danger and felt strongly to pray for her daughter, who happened to be in an automobile accident and almost went off a cliff. Her daughter experienced injuries, but was saved from a fatal accident. Mrs. Dobson's sensitivity to the prompting of the Holy Spirit to pray saved her daughter from disaster.

My daughter led us into an evening of prophetic intercession one Saturday night. We sang songs and spoke God's Word over each other. It was an amazing night where the Holy Spirit met us. Vickie repeatedly spoke **Psalm 91:1: "He that dwells in the secret place of the most high shall abide under the shadow of the almighty."**

The next day our son was south on I-25 heading home in snowy conditions and a vehicle cut in front of him. To avoid hitting the vehicle, he lost control on a patch of ice and rolled the vehicle. Amazingly, he crawled out of the vehicle with a scratch on his finger and maybe a slight concussion. When the police arrived, they asked where the driver was and could not believe he was the driver based on the condition of the vehicle. They had witnessed many similar scenes that were not so good for the driver and passengers. The vehicle was a total loss, but our son made it out with only a scratch, praise God. I believe the prayers and praise the night before kept my son safe.

Elevating Moment:

I recently witnessed an amazing miracle and I am still surprised by what my eyes witnessed. All I can say is we serve an awesome and living God. A miracle I had never seen or experienced before. I was on the golf course in Newland, NC. Max and Martha invited me to play golf. My wife and I celebrated our twenty-seventh wedding anniversary for the week and she agreed with me to join our new friends for golf. As we enjoyed the fellowship and challenge of keeping a good golf score, Martha began instructing me where to hit the golf ball as we approached the eighteenth hole. In the meanwhile, Martha's husband Max turned the golf cart around to pick up Martha. Unaware of what each other was doing, Martha quickly turned around into the path of the golf cart, and her husband accidently hit her. She fell to the ground. I saw Martha's face and knew she was in excruciating pain as she began to grasp her leg. I looked at her leg, which appeared to be broken and terribly disfigured. Immediately, I prayed, "In the name of Jesus, no broken bones, no torn ligaments, in Jesus' name."

I blinked my eyes wondering if my eyes saw what I had witnessed. As I prayed, her leg appeared to change as though veins began to reconnect and bones were put back in place. Martha asked to be placed in the golf cart and as we sat her in, she looked at me as though she was astonished. She said, "There is no more pain!"

I told her husband to get her to the hospital. When they arrived at their home, she was able to walk on her leg with no pain, and said, "God gave me a miracle." She knew her leg had been broken. All I could do was cry because of God's amazing mercy. I witnessed a creative miracle right before my eyes! I believe God wants to empower His people, but we must align with God's agenda and cooperate with the Holy Spirit.

So why do we need the Baptism in the Holy Spirit? It's simple: we must be empowered with boldness to witness to those who are lost and to overcome sinful desires.

In my salvation experience, I accepted Christ at age twelve. I truly loved God and wanted to obey God in everything, but felt absent of power to overcome sin. I failed miserably and repeatedly as a young believer. I believe I disobeyed the Word of God more than I obeyed. I beat myself up and the devil flooded my mind with condemnation. I went back to God each time to ask His forgiveness. At the age of twenty-one, I received the baptism of the Holy Spirit, with the evidence of speaking in a heavenly language. I had, for the first time, power to be a bold witness for Jesus. I still had problems and challenges to deal with, but I had more victories than failures once I received the baptism of the Holy Spirit.

Just as a car has to be filled with fuel when it becomes low from use, the principle applies that we must go back to God and get filled up on a daily basis. If we don't exercise the Word in our life and stay filled with the Holy Spirit, we are capable of doing the things we did before we came into the knowledge of Christ. Why take a chance missing vital moments with the Lord. Redeem the time for the days are evil.

Acts 1:8: "Power for service; but you shall receive power after the Holy Ghost has come upon you. Power to overcome sin and live a victorious life."

Romans 8:26: "Likewise the Spirit also helps in our weaknesses. For we do not know what we should pray for as we ought, but the Spirit Himself makes intercession for us with groaning's which cannot be uttered."

Luke 24:49: "Behold, I send the promise of my father upon you; but tarry or remain in the city of Jerusalem until you are endued with power from on high."

Acts 9:17-20 states empowerment comes through God's ordained vessels. Paul was empowered by Ananias. Acts 10:38 states Jesus was powered by the Holy Spirit as well.

If you desire all of God's fullness, the answer for you and me should be a resounding "yes." I say this because I needed power to be an effective witness for Christ. I faced temptations in school and did not have the will power to overcome until I was filled with power from the Holy Spirit. People refuse this gift; I believe it's because they can't figure out how the Holy Spirit works in our lives. One's intellect blocks a person from receiving. God clearly says to us that the Holy Spirit will guide us into all truth. **Hebrews 11:6 says, "But without faith it is impossible to please Him, for he who comes to God must believe that He is, and that He is a rewarder of those who diligently seek Him."**

Prayer Elevating Moment:

Ask God to guide you and to help you freely accept all He has and intends for you. **Pray this prayer**: "If the Baptism in the Holy Spirit is something I should have, I fully receive it now in Jesus' name." To refuse tongues is to refuse to yield completely to God. If you will not yield completely, you cannot be used completely. Now, I realize some individuals have misused this gift as saying they are more spiritually mature, but that is not what this is about. This is about being a powerful witness for Christ.

I would like to use another football analogy. When I played football in high school, I was a decent player with decent ability, but to get better and more effective, I knew I had to train and prepare more. I also knew I would have to develop my speed, so we were encouraged by our coaches to run track. After a few track seasons, my speed was greatly enhanced. Attaining breakaway speed set me a part to be a more explosive and powerful football player. This hard work and effort won me a full football scholarship. This opportunity didn't happen because I was sitting around; it took desire, determination and discipline.

You probably wonder what this has to do with living a spirit-filled life. The point here is we have to put forth effort in seeking the things of God. Yes, we know God freely gives this gift to all His children. Therefore, we should freely receive all His gifts as little children receive gifts from their parents. The gift to run fast was in me and I had a desire to develop this speed. To be a more excellent athlete, this 4.2-second speed had to be activated. It was activated because I was hungry to grow and to be more effective. In my sports career days we said to each other, **"You got to believe. You got to want it."**

Every Christ follower has the Holy Spirit in him/her. The difference is when you are baptized in the Holy Spirit, God pours power into you and you will have a direct power connection with heaven. This power helps you move into super human or supernatural ability to be used of God. The bottom line: you have to want more of God and you must believe God's Word and you will receive the gift of the spirit in evidence by speaking in a heavenly language. Get downright hungry for more of God.

Luke 11:13: "If you then being evil, know how to give good gifts to your children, how much more will your heavenly Father give the Holy Spirit to those who ask Him!"

Matthew 5:6: "Blessed are those who hunger and thirst for righteousness for they shall be filled."

Important Point: If you have ever involved yourself in spiritual activities that were outside the boundaries of God's Word, you must first renounce any evil forms of witchcraft and occult in Jesus' name and cover yourself in the blood of Jesus. Also, ask the Holy Spirit to reveal any areas that Satan could have gotten a foothold in your life without your knowledge. This obviously is new subject matter that may require getting spiritual counsel from a pastor or leader who can better explain how to overcome these strongholds (Deuteronomy 18:10-12, Acts 19:19).

How to receive the baptism of the Holy Spirit? **Acts 19:6: "And when Paul had laid hands on them, the Holy Spirit came upon them and they spoke with tongues and prophesied."** When a leader who understands the working and moving of the Holy Spirit lays hands on someone, it facilitates the process.

Acts 10:44-46:

> While Peter was still speaking these words; the Holy Spirit fell upon all those who heard the word. Those of the circumcision who believed were astonished, as many as came with Peter, because the gift of the Holy Spirit had been poured out on the gentiles also. For they heard them speak with tongues and magnify God.

The focus must be on Jesus. Raise your hands in true worship unto the Lord. Closed eyes help shield from distraction, allowing your thoughts and your mind to dwell on Jesus. Ask for the promise of the Father and praise the name of Jesus. God will not force you to speak in tongues. It is a voluntary act of speaking what you hear in your spirit. As the Lord places words in your mind, speak them out boldly. Speak and repeat what you hear. The Spirit will give you more words. The new language, which the Spirit has given you, is not only a sign of the initial reception of the gift of the Spirit, but also of His continuing presence. **1 Corinthians 14:4: "He who speaks in a tongue edifies himself, but he who prophesies edifies the church."** When you receive your heavenly language, it keeps you built up to have power to handle temptations and power to share Jesus with individuals. **Jude 1:20: "But you beloved building yourselves up on your most holy faith, praying in the Holy Spirit."**

1 Corinthians 12:1-11 gives us a list of gifts of the Spirit. These are power tools to advance God's kingdom:

1. **Word of wisdom:** supernatural revelation given of God's direction and guidance for a specific situation.

2. **Word of knowledge**: a revelation of a piece of information which cannot be known in a natural way; God's diagnosis of a problem, a sickness or other situation.

3. **The gift of faith:** Assurance of God's ability to act in a given situation. Faith cancels doubt.

4. **Gifts of healing**: a special anointing of the Holy Spirit, which enables us to bring healing, God's healing power to those who are sick.

5. **Working of miracles**: a special momentary gift of authority, which enables us to perform miracles in Jesus' name.

6. **Discerning of spirits:** a supernatural gift which enables us to discern the difference between the Holy Spirit, the human's spirit and evil spirits. It is not the discerning of character or faults.

7. **Gift of prophecy:** an anointing of the Holy Spirit to speak the words of God. It is always for direction, up-building and encouragement. Sometimes it may be for predicting future events, if God wants us to know them.

8. **Gift of tongues:** a supernatural means for God's communication with His people. It is a message given in a language unknown to the speaker and always used in conjunction with the gift of interpretation.

9. **Gift of interpretation of tongues:** gives back in one's language the meaning of what was said in the gift of tongues. These two gifts operating together are equivalent to prophecy.

Bottom line: the foundation of these gifts is love manifesting the love of God to people.

In closing this important chapter, I find it encouraging that God spoke to Ananias to pray and lay hands on Saul. Ananias laid hands on him and he received sight and was filled with the Holy Spirit.

Acts 9:17-18:

> **And Ananias went his way and entered the house; and laying his hands on him he said, "Brother Saul, the Lord Jesus who appeared to you on the road as you came has sent me that you may receive your sight and be filled with the Holy Spirit." Immediately there fell from his eyes something like scales, and he received his sight at once and he arose and was baptized.**

Acts 19:1-5 :

> **Paul because obviously empowered by the Holy Spirit and went about empowering others believers as well. And it happened, while Apollos was at Corinth, that Paul, having passed through the upper regions, came to Ephesus. And finding some disciples he said to them. "Did you receive the Holy Spirit when you believed?" So they said to him, "We have not so much as heard whether there is a Holy Spirit." And he said to them, "Into what then were you baptized?" So they said Into John's baptism." Then Paul said, "John indeed baptized with a baptism of repentance, saying to the people that they should believe on Him who would come after him, that is, on Christ Jesus." When they heard this, they were baptized in the name of the Lord Jesus. And when Paul laid hands on them, the Holy Spirit came upon them, and they spoke with tongues and prophesied.**

Christ followers need power in the days to come to elevate above the chaos of the world's problems. We will need the power of the Holy Spirit in our life. Don't close your heart to God's Holy Word and allow what you have been taught from your past to deter you from receiving all God wants you to have. The word clearly says the Holy Spirit will guide you into all truth.

Step Six: Ready

Numbers 14:24

"But my servant Caleb has a different attitude than the others have. He has remained loyal to me, so I will bring him into the Land he explored. His descendants will possess their full share of that Land."

R eady means completely prepared or in fit condition for immediate action. To elevate to your destiny requires a different level of thinking. With that new level of thinking comes a readiness to receive instruction and confidence to accomplish great exploits for God. When you understand and see from God's view, you know what you are able to accomplish through God.

I vividly remember being in the eleventh grade in class with a teammate, Delton Hall, who was a senior who went on to Clemson and later played with the Pittsburgh Steelers. Another teammate, Reuben Davis, went to the University of North Carolina, Chapel Hill, and later played with the San Diego Chargers. We were pulled aside by school officials and they explained to us that in order to attend college we had to have specific classes successfully completed, specific SAT scores, and maintain positive behavior. I noticed we had opportunities coming our way and we had to do our part to be ready for each opportunity. I began to study and work hard, clearly recognizing God gave me favor.

I remember one Saturday spring morning preparing to take the SAT and feeling nervous. I knew my going to college hinged on how well I performed on the nationwide test. This test was key to being positioned to enter this new level in my journey. Looking back, I know it was God who gave me the desire and ability to succeed. I made the required score to get into college on the first try. I know I am what I am by the grace of God. In my senior season of high school, I met all requirements for college and I was offered multiple scholarships in football and track, to God be the glory!

I like how the legendary coach John Wooden stated, "When opportunity comes, it is too late to prepare." We all need to be ready when God sized opportunities come our way. The key to being ready is to stay in prayer, stay in the Word and pray in your heavenly language.

In a practical sense, being ready is not to procrastinate duties that can be done today so you are ready when elevating moments come your way.

Because Caleb often communed with the Lord, he had confidence to conquer any giant because he knew he served an awesome and capable Lord. Caleb had a different attitude because of his connection with God. When you have dwelt close to God's presence or have been in proximity to God, there is a transfer of confidence.

When we have followed God's instructions, we become qualified and useful for God's service. One aspect of being ready is having your armor on. As mentioned in the section on authority, Ephesians 6:10-18 gives us precise details in being ready at a moment's notice.

I also think about the five out of ten virgins who had their lamps full and were ready when the Lord came. Prayer helps keep our tanks and lamps full. This is a clear example of how each person is responsible for being ready and having fresh oil for themselves every day (Matthew 25:1-13). I have discovered when I have spent time in prayer and read the Word of God I am much more equipped to handle the matters that come my way. One will receive much more meat when we move through scriptures studying text looking up meaning in Hebrew and Greek.

2 Samuel 5:24: "And it shall be, when you hear the sound of marching in the tops of the mulberry trees, then you shall advance quickly. For then the Lord will go out before you to strike the camp of the Philistines." David had to be ready to respond to God's instruction in order to achieve victory. Prayer prepares us to respond, in a timely fashion, to bring about victory and overthrow the enemy's tactics and plans. "The law of timing" God gives us are windows of opportunity we must advance through quickly. Prayer helps us hear God's instruction to align for victory in our lives. The Greek meaning for *kairos* is "the right or opportune moment;" another meaning is "a time when conditions are right for the accomplishment of a crucial action; the opportune and decisive moment."

Tools to engage in prayer:

Confessions to speak over myself:

1. I am in the perfect will of God. (Jeremiah 29:11)

2. I am blessed to be a blessing (Genesis 12:2).

3. I know the voice of the Good Shepherd. (John 10:14)

4. The Word is working mightily in me. (Hebrews 11:6)

5. I am enjoying all the benefits of the Spirit-filled life. (Acts 1:8)

Rules of engagement

Prayer of authority:

I decree and declare the eyes of my spirit function with 20/20 vision for correct understanding and interpretation of divine movements. My ears are in tune with the correct frequency of the Spirit and I have clear transmission. (2 Kings 6:17, Psalm 119:18, Isaiah 29:18, Jeremiah 1:11-16, 2 Corinthians 4:4, Ephesians 4:18, Revelation 4:1)

How does God speak to us?

*   God speaks to us through His Word which is called the *logos,* the written word. **2Timothy 3:16-17 says, *"All Scripture is given by inspiration of God and is profitable for doctrine, reproof, correction, and instruction in righteousness. That the man of God may be perfect and thoroughly furnished unto all good works."*** God's word improves our life and builds strong character within us.

God's Word cultivates a healthy mind and builds strong morals. God's Word helps us correct mistakes and curb our passions.

* God gives a *rhema* word, which in Greek means "an utterance, a portion of scripture that speaks to a believer in a current situation." This is where a portion of scripture speaks directly to and is custom fit for the circumstance you are currently facing (1 Corinthians 2:12-13).

* God speaks through His servants as we see with Ananias in **Acts 9:17: "And Ananias went his way and entered the house; and laying his hands on him he said, 'Brother Saul, the Lord Jesus who appeared to you on the road as you came, has sent me that you may receive your sight and be filled with the Holy Spirit.'"**

* Jesus also speaks in an audible voice as with Saul in **Acts 9:6:** *"So he, trembling and astonished, said, 'Lord, what do You want me to do?' Then the Lord said to him, 'Arise and go into the city, and you will be told what you must do.'"* I believe God appears to a person on this level due to the magnitude of the call, as with Moses at the burning bush. The greater the revelation, the greater the responsibility.

* God speaks to us in our dreams and gives visions. As we read in **Daniel 2:22-30:**

> **He reveals deep and secret things; He knows what is in the darkness, And light dwells with Him. I thank You and praise You O God of my fathers; You have given me wisdom and might, And have now made known to me what we asked of You, For You have made known to us the king's demand. Therefore Daniel went to Arioch, whom the king had appointed to destroy the**

wise men of Babylon. He went and said thus to him: "Do not destroy the wise men of Babylon; take me before the king, and I will tell the king the interpretation."

Then Arioch quickly brought Daniel before the king, and said thus to him, "I have found a man of the captives of Judah, who will make known to the king the interpretation."

The king answered and said to Daniel, whose name was Belteshazzar, "Are you able to make known to me the dream which I have seen, and its interpretation?"

Daniel answered in the presence of the king, and said, "The secret which the king has demanded, the wise men, the astrologers, the magicians, and the soothsayers cannot declare to the king. But there is a God in heaven who reveals secrets, and He has made known to King Nebuchadnezzar what will be in the latter days. Your dream, and the visions of your head upon your bed, were these: As for you, O king, thoughts came to your mind while on your bed, about what would come to pass after this; and He who reveals secrets has made known to you what will be. But as for me, this secret has not been revealed to me because I have more wisdom than anyone living, but for our sakes who make known the interpretation to the king, and that you may know the thoughts of your heart."

As we dwell in the light of God's Word and the light of His presence He will reveal deep secrets to us. The price for these amazing insights is paid by the time we spend with the Lord. If we cannot schedule daily time with God, we need to admit our relationship to God is not one of our highest priorities. If this is true, spiritual disaster could be right around the corner (understanding prayer). As we observe in this text, if Daniel had not received an answer from God, they would die.

1 Corinthians 2:9-16:

But as it is written: Eye has not seen, nor ear heard, Nor have entered into the heart of man The things which God has prepared for those who love Him. But God has revealed them to us through His Spirit. For the Spirit searches all things, yes, the deep things of God. For what man knows the things of a man except the spirit of the man which is in him? Even so no one knows the things of God except the Spirit of God. Now we have received, not the spirit of the world, but the Spirit who is from God, that we might know the things that have been freely given to us by God. These things we also speak, not in words which man's wisdom teaches but which the Holy Spirit teaches, comparing spiritual things with spiritual. But the natural man does not receive the things of the Spirit of God, for they are foolishness to him; nor can he know them, because they are spiritually discerned. But he who is spiritual judges all things, yet he himself is rightly judged by no one. For who has known the mind of the Lord that he may instruct Him? But we have the mind of Christ.

God's purpose is revealed to us by the Spirit of God.

Step Seven: Strategy

1 Samuel 30:8

"Then David asked the Lord, 'Should I chase after this band of raiders? Will I catch them?' And the Lord told him, 'Yes, go after them. You will surely recover everything that was taken from you.'"

Strategy means, "High level plan to achieve one or more goals." I believe we need to plan our day and be flexible if the Holy Spirit directs another way. **Proverbs 16:9 says, "A man's heart plans his way but, the Lord directs his steps."** The best strategy is to go to God first. I recall a strategy God spoke to me concerning my position as a young distribution supervisor. I was had many challenges with safety, attendance, attitude and production on all three shifts. I took matters to prayer and the Lord revealed to me that I needed to walk around the entire warehouse and pray daily. In times of prayer, I began to see how to solve these problems. "With safety, reinforce with workers safety procedures; organize all machinery in one area by number, so that employees know exactly where to find their machines." This effort took the cooperation of all three shifts. At the end of each shift, I recognized those who made or exceeded their quota. This strategy from the Lord worked. We had fewer accidents and more efficiency in the transition from one shift to another because employees knew exactly where to go to find their machinery. Moral was better and employees wanted to achieve and exceed their goals.

Matthew 7:7-8: "Keep on asking, and you will receive what you ask for. Keep on seeking, and you will find. Keep on knocking, and the door will be opened to you. For everyone who asks, receives. Everyone who seeks finds. And to everyone who knocks, the door will be opened." Here we clearly see if we ask according to His will, we will receive. Knocking symbolizes a consistency and hunger for the things of God. God has promised to fill us when we are thirsty and hungry.

Luke 6:12 (NLT): "One day soon afterward Jesus went up on a mountain to pray and he prayed to God all night." When we have to make difficult decisions we need the mind of God. If we wait, God will download a plan to help us overcome (David and the Philistines: David consistently went to God for instruction and strategy). **Mark 6:46-47:**

> **After telling everyone good-bye, he went up into the hills by himself to pray. And when even was come, the ship was in the midst of the sea, and he was alone on the land. Jesus had special times of prayer with the father right before confronting the need to demonstrate His power over Nature.**

Elevating Moment:

I recall when Vickie and I purchased our second home in Colorado Springs in 1998. We were so thrilled to see the house built from the ground up. Periodically we went over and prayed over the property and saw how much was accomplished. When the house was completed we had to pick colors, appliances, cabinets and the type of carpet. Vickie was so thrilled, however, when we went over to see the progress we discovered that the company had ordered and installed the wrong carpet. Light gray is what we chose, but the builder installed pink carpet throughout the entire house. My wife Vickie was obviously upset, to put it lightly. What made matters even worse was they refused to change the carpet out for the correct color. Vickie and I prayed for wisdom in how to proceed. God in His faithfulness gave Vickie the strategy for success. She acted upon the strategy from the Lord and behold, the next day they came and changed all the carpet at no extra expense to us and made apologies for the error. Praise God for divine strategy.

In the book of 2 Timothy 3:1-6, we are clearly told what kind of times we will face. Like never before we certainly need to elevate our prayer life. **1 Timothy 3:1-6 (NLT):**

> **You should know this, Timothy, that in the last days there will be very difficult times. For people will love only themselves and their money. They will be boastful and proud, scoffing at God, disobedient to their parents, and ungrateful. They will consider nothing sacred. They will be unloving and unforgiving; they will slander others and have no self-control. They will be**

cruel and hate what is good. They will betray their friends, be reckless, be puffed up with pride, and love pleasure rather than God. They will act religious, but they will reject the power that could make them godly. Stay away from people like that! They are the kind who work their way into people's homes and win the confidence of vulnerable women who are burdened with the guilt of sin and controlled by various desires.

So we see several factors that will be common in the latter times.

Seven reasons to elevate your prayer life:

1. Times will be difficult, therefore, elevate your prayer life to walk in God's peace.

2. People will be selfish and self-centered. We need to elevate our prayer so we can avoid this attitude.

3. People will be full of pride. We need to stay in God to remain humble.

4. People will be unthankful, therefore, elevate prayer to keep a heart of gratitude.

5. People will be unloving and hateful. We have to elevate our prayer to avoid the spirit of hate.

6. People will act as if they know Christ, but deny the power of God. We must elevate our prayer so we can stay close to the power of God and be led by the Holy Spirit.

7. People will be weak, laden with many problems and weak men acting in self-ishness will take advantage of women for their own pleasure. Therefore, we must elevate our prayer life so we can protect the innocent and weak in our society and world.

Elevating Moment:

In 1992, I was faced with a dilemma as a young textile supervisor. I was told not to conduct Bible studies at work during my break times. I was also told not to give out invitations to church and I complied. Then I was told not use the name of Jesus on the job and not to speak about Jesus. I in turn said, "In the distribution center employees and supervisors use all types of language and inappropriate language, so why am I been censored?" The shift I led was the most productive and efficient of the three shifts. We accomplished more work with fewer workers than the first shift. My role as supervisor and getting the job done was not the issue. The issue was Christ influenced the people who worked for me.

Here's an example of the impact of Christ. One employee decided to get married instead of continuing to be in a "shacking up" situation. Another employee became involved in the church. God touched lives and the devil did not like it. So the ultimatum was stop talking about Jesus or be fired. I went back to the shift knowing that night would be my last.

When I arrived home, I began to ponder. Maybe I am a little too radical. I then heard the Holy Spirit instruct me to go to **Psalm 71:15-24:**

My mouth will tell your acts of loving kindness and Your salvation all the day, for I do not know their numbers. I shall go in the strength of Adonai, the Lord. I shall make mention of Your acts of loving kindness, of Yours only. O God, You have taught me from my youth, and to now I have declared Your wondrous works. Now also when I am old and grey headed,

O God, Do not forsake me until I have shown Your strength to this generation, Your power to each one that is come! Your acts of loving kindness also, God, are very high, Who has done great things. O God, who is like You? You, Who has shown me great and severe troubles, will quicken me again and will bring me up again from the depths of the earth. You will increase my greatness and comfort me on every side. I shall also praise You with the psaltery. Your truth, my God. I shall sing to You with the harp, O You, Holy one of Israel. My lips will greatly rejoice when I sing praises to you. You have redeemed my life. My tongue also will talk of your acts of loving kindness all day long, for they are confounded, for those who seek my hurt are brought to shame.

I also received a call from a friend of ours, named Trudie, confirming God's Word and instruction to me. This portion of scripture was a *rhema* word and was backed up by a prophetic word from Trudie. Because of this clear instruction I was able to go to work with confidence and do what the Lord instructed me. I was called into the office by the personnel manager and the department manager. They asked me what I had decided. I stated, "I will not initiate a conversation about Jesus. However, if someone asks the question, I would answer concerning Jesus."

Keep in mind we were in a fast-paced environment. There was not much time to talk until the work was done. They knew this issue was not work. The real issue was Jesus! They became annoyed I did not consent to stop speaking about

Jesus. They asked me questions, such as, "By what authority do you think you can do this?"

I said, "In Jesus' name."

Then they said, "We attend church; why are you so radical about Jesus?"

I said, "I would not be here if it were not for Jesus saving me. Jesus gave me this job. I just can't stop talking about Jesus, who I love."

Then the personnel manager said, "When we hired you, it was a highlight of my career. We will have to let you go."

I stood up, shook their hands and thanked them for the opportunity to work for this company. I told them I had learned a lot and thanked them for giving me the opportunity. Then, I said good-bye. As our culture becomes more and more antagonistic to Christ, we must be prepared and equipped to handle the antichrist spirit.

Closing

Christ followers, we must ready ourselves because there is an assault on our freedoms and families. As you align in prayer with God and His agenda, the Lord will help you see what is being planned to destroy the freedoms we enjoy. Let us not take for granted the freedom we have to read God's Word and to pray in public unto our Father. **Isaiah 55:6: "Seek the Lord while he may be found, call upon Him while He is near."** I can boldly say prayer has saved my life from destruction, saved my marriage from disaster, and prayer has helped me recognize I cannot adequately be the father I need to be to my children without God's grace and wisdom. Prayer has sustained me to walk worthy of the vocation that I have been called to. Prayer has been a lifestyle that I want to see grow among family, friends and Christ followers. When we spend time with God, we elevate our thinking because God said His ways are higher than our ways and His thoughts higher than our thoughts.

Isaiah 55:8-9: in order to elevate in God, we have to elevate our thinking. The reason I wrote this book is simply to encourage Christ followers all around the globe to elevate their prayer life, to be alert and effective in winning souls for Jesus and advancing God's work. We need unity within the body of Christ. God said in Psalm 133:1-3:

Behold, how good it is for brethren to dwell together in unity! It is like the precious oil upon the head, running down on the beard of Aaron running down on the edge of his garments. It is like the dew of Hermon, descending upon the mountains of Zion; for there the Lord commanded the blessing life forevermore.

I like what Paul said in **Colossians 1:9: "For this cause we also, since the day we heard. I, do not cease to pray for you, and to desire that you might be filled with the knowledge of His will in all wisdom and spiritual understanding."**

We must stay connected to God to get divine communication!

Proverbs 29:18: "Where there is no vision, divine guidance, or revelation the people run wild, cast off restraint. But, happy is he who keeps the law."

Vision means *chazown* in Hebrew ("divine communication"). We are in a war; we need daily divine communication with God, fresh bread for the new day ahead. Vision here refers to service to God. God unveils His awesome plan for your life. Some grab it. Some miss it. Prayer and cooperation give you the ability to grab it.

Perish: The Hebrew meaning is *para*, which means loose, ignore, avoid, neglect to loosen restraint, and show lack of restraint.

Keep: Hebrew meaning is *shamar*, to guard and protect. Before we thought about a Destiny Project in 1997, I was up on a mountain in Colorado Springs seeking and praising God. God began to down load a strategy to me regarding effectively reaching young people. I was so excited and felt so empowered by God's awesome presence. The presence of God was so real that I felt it was a heavy presence. After receiving the strategy, I began to climb down the mountain and once I reached the bottom, I began to rationalize. "I can't do that and I don't know how to do what God put on my heart." I decided to put it on the shelf; the next day in the church service Cindy Jacobs, author, speaker and founder of General International, spoke prophetically to us exactly what God showed me on the mountain. Then I realized God is serious about the "destiny strategies" He gave me on the mountain.

Vickie and I began to move forward with the plans. Seventeen years later, we are developing leaders to lead sites across the United States. God said in **Jeremiah 29:11: "'For I know the plans I have for you,' says the Lord. 'They are plans for good and not disaster to give you a future and a hope.'"** When we realize how much God values each of us as well as how much He wants to do through us, we will cooperate with the Holy Spirit on a consistent basis. Value means worth and importance. You are of great worth and importance to God. So get in the war, pray and obey.

Daniel understood his value. He also understood the importance of a life set apart for God. Daniel made the decisions that positioned him to be better. He also had the determination to live holy because he knew his destiny would be greatness. He knew this because he spent time with God.

"Know" in Hebrew is *yada*, to know and learn. Daniel was willing to know God intimately and learn how to hear from God. Daniel knew if they prayed, God would give them a plan. Plan in Hebrew is *machhasbah*, purpose. Daniel also knew God's plans are good. The word good in Hebrew is *shalom,* which means completeness, soundness, safety, health, peace and friendship. When we choose our own way, we are bound to experience disaster. Disaster in Hebrew is *ra,* meaning evil, distress, misery, injury and calamity. God does not desire for you to be in misery; God wants to give us an awesome destiny and an outcome that is good.

Isaiah 46:10: "Only I can tell you the future before it happens. Everything I plan will come to pass, for I do whatever I wish." We must realize our plans may be good, but God's plan is the best plan. God knows the outcome. The word "tell" in Hebrew, *nagad*, is mentioned 222 times in the Bible. What is God telling you to do today? My question to you is, what has God advised you about? The best way to get clarification is to schedule time alone with God. Only God's purpose will be established, stand the test of time, rise and endure.

The basis for the numbers Isaiah 22:22 and Daniel 2:22: the numbers 222 indicate shifting a grid, aligning your thoughts with God's so you can complete your life's purpose. 222 also means light in **Psalm 119:105: "Thy word is a lamp unto**

my feet and a light unto my path." God orchestrates every step if we follow the Holy Spirit. The Holy Spirit guides the way to truth of the Word.

The past two years I have involved myself with prayer initiatives with the National Day of Prayer (NDP) right before I departed for Israel in December 2013. I was told the NDP sought a volunteer coordinator for Colorado. I thought about the possibility, but dismissed the idea due to my busy schedule. When the Lord brought my life to a halt due to knee surgery, He began to impress and stir my heart something He wanted to do. I was not sure exactly what, but I knew something was on the horizon.

My good friends invited me over to the national office. My goal was to get input on writing this book on prayer. What I did not know was that they would ask me to pray about being the Colorado state coordinator. I must say I was surprised and said I would pray about this role. In my mind, I did not feel qualified or equipped to mobilize prayer for the entire state of Colorado. As I sought the Lord, He impressed me with Nehemiah 4:14. However, I did not have peace about taking on such a tremendous responsibility. I continued to pray and talk to my staff and family. No one in my family or staff could see how I could add something more to my plate.

My wife said something profound: "You may not have room in your schedule, but if God is telling you to do this, you have no options but to obey the Lord."

I can honestly say I appreciated those words of my wife, but I still did not have peace. One morning I decided I would join the twenty-one days of prayer at the World Prayer Center. I hobbled over there with my two crutches as I did when I went for a visit at NDP a few days prior. I sat down in a place called "the furnace."

In constant prayer and worship, I read my Bible, nodded a few times, listened and sang worship songs. One particular song hit my spirit and caused me to tear-up and weep. The song said, "In this season will you obey me." I knew then I had to obey and peace came to me to walk into this door.

When God opens a door, things happen fast and within weeks of accepting the NDP role, I planned a convocation at the World Prayer Center inviting all inter-cessors and prayer leaders. The date of the convocation was February 22, 2014. The numbers 222 stayed in my forefront, confirming from heaven that I was on the right path. I continued to see these numbers to the point that I knew they were not a coincidence. This number was everywhere from traveling on highways 122, 221, 220 getting off on exits with numbers 222. These numbers indicated God's light and path; the numbers are a sign of light to align with my soul's purpose.

If we are honest with ourselves, we are ready and willing to accept all of God's blessings and protection. However, do we desire His will, which involves dying to our agenda, and making time with Him our number one priority? If we want to spend time with God, then it will reflect in how we start and spend our day. Does our day start with Him, and is it about Him, and does it end with Him? Or is your day without Him, starts without Him? Do you not think about what He wants and we instead focus on our own desires? God want us to find pleasure in Him and enjoy life to the fullest.

Daniel demonstrated to us a life of purpose and a life focused on God. He received divine communication that saved him and others. Daniel experienced protection from plots against him, and ferocious lions. In Daniel 2:22, **"He reveals**

deep and mysterious things and knows what lies hidden in darkness, though he is surrounded by light."

2 Timothy 2:2: "And the things that you have heard from me among many witnesses, commit these to faithful men who will be able to teach others also." The revelation that God gives us must be shared with discretion as Paul tells Timothy to faithful men.

Isaiah 22:22: "The key of the house of David I will lay on his shoulder, so he shall open and no one shall shut and no one shall open." I have often tried to open doors for myself, but I have learned as we rest and wait on God, He opens the doors He wants us to enter. We too often become impatient and move before God's timing. As we grow in our faith we learn God's timing is the best time and has the most fruitful results.

Vickie has had a desire to travel to Israel since she was fifteen years old. Her opportunity came when she was fifty years old. Vickie and I, for the first time in our life, were given an opportunity to travel to Israel with a group of pastors and leaders facilitated by Christians United for Israel. Vickie and I flew into Washington, D.C. and stayed with her brother who lives in Maryland. Then we rented a car to drive up to New Jersey and met the rest of the team at a hotel. This was an amazing opportunity to travel with leaders I once worked with when I was youth pastor for Pastor Otis Lockett, Sr. We departed on a cold December morning in 2013 and arrived into Tel Aviv ten hours later. It was the smoothest flight I have ever been on. The airline was El Al, an Israeli airline that honors the Sabbath. When we touched ground we immediately began touring Israel. Visiting Caesarea, Masada, the Dead Sea, the Sea of Galilee, and later that evening we went to the

Wailing Wall. The best way I can explain what we experienced is my body, mind and spirit were on overload with electric power. Vickie was so impacted that she was speechless for nearly three hours. Our time in the holy land was one we will never forget. We felt like we were home, walking where Jesus walked, and experiencing the Bible firsthand.

God bless you and remember: *Elevate to Your Destiny.*

Reference Page:

For God's Sake Rest! by James L. Anderson

Change Agent by O.S. Hillman

Smith Wigglesworth Complete collection

Prayers for Everyday by Burt Bjorklund

Dr. Hilda Britain Pamphlet

Tommy Burchfield Confessions

Rules of Engagement by Cindy Trim

CPSIA information can be obtained
at www.ICGtesting.com
Printed in the USA
LVOW03s2120080516

487281LV00005B/13/P